Endorsements

I just happen to know this author personally. Jenn Stockman is indescribable. Every attempt will fall short. Trying to pinpoint her down is like sailing out to the center of the Pacific Ocean and dropping a penny overboard, waiting a month and then driving down to find it. You'd discover so much more before you ever found that penny. But, when you read her writing, you begin to see what I am trying to say. Nobody sees Jenn coming! Every time we cross paths in recent years, she has transformed some part of herself into someone you didn't even know was in there. She is young so this is just going to be a phenomenal unfolding.

Hiding in the pages of *The War on Your Voice* is a personal tour guide. This guide will lead you to places that you didn't even know you had. You are about to discover cisterns in your heart that were sealed away like Tut's tomb. Be prepared to find riches and glory beyond your wildest imagination that God is so thrilled to give you as you follow the guidance of a masterful writer. I highly recommend this book to you and pray for your victory in winning the war on your voice.

Danny Silk
President of Loving On Purpose Life Academy
Senior Leader Teams of Bethel Church, Redding, CA & Jesus Culture, Sacramento
Author of *Keep Your Love On* & *Culture of Honor*

Wow, I just began to read the introduction and felt the presence of God fall! I was moved to tears not just by Jenn's writing but by the Weighty Presence that accompanies her words. *The War on Your Voice* is not just another book on freedom, it is an impartation. Jenn's victories in overcoming fear and accessing God's presence and freedom, have given her great authority and grace to impart new hope and freedom for her readers. Jenn carries an anointing to impart life-changing nuggets of truth that will change your life. I highly recommend this book and its author.

Wendy Backlund

Author of *Victorious Emotions* and *Living from the Unseen*

There are few things more inspiring than a life lived with passionate clarity, the life Jenn Stockman models. To know Jenn is to be acquainted with honor, spiritual hunger and humility. *The War on Your Voice* is a must read for anyone desiring to personally experience the exhilaration of life fully lived!

Leif Hetland

President

Global Mission Awareness

Author of *Called To Reign*

The War on Your Voice is a book so full of life giving words – yes – written, vocal words! Jenn has a life testimony of loving- forgiving and giving room for those around her to find their voice and to encourage them in their personal journeys with the Father. I'm proud to be her family's "Georgia grandma."

Jennifer Hetland

Mom, Author, Friend

Inside each of us is a longing to know who we truly are. Knowing and embracing our identity is the key to living life as fully as God intended. God's heart for us is true freedom, knowing who we were created to be and what He thinks about us. Jenn Stockman's voice has been raised up to reveal the heart of the Father to a generation that desperately struggles with their identity. In *The War On Your Voice*, Jenn eloquently and powerfully invites us on a journey to experience the revelation of who we are in God and discover the heart of the Father. It is this revelation that brings us the freedom Jesus paid a great price for us to live in.

Banning Liebscher
Jesus Culture Founder and Pastor

I love Jenn Stockman with my whole heart!! She is the real deal. She is such a lover of Jesus and people. She carries His heart. We have been friends since we were young and I've watched her pastor and teach so beautifully. She's an amazing mom and wife.

Jenn Johnson
Bethel Music

Jenn has a significant and provoking message of validation, value and the power of your unique voice. I can feel her strength and kindness as she opens up the deep, vulnerable and real places of her story. This is such a relevant topic for many and I believe that the words in these pages will lead us into new territories of freedom and promise. Get ready to be inspired and challenged.

Candace Johnson
Senior Leader, Bethel Redding

In the early 2000's was when I first met Jenn. Over the years she has become one of my closest friends. The relationship she shares with Father God has brought so much life to me personally. Her message is one that calls us into a place of abandonment and truth. I have watched Jenn navigate life through mountains and valleys, and her heart posture to Jesus is yes. Yes to the surrender, yes to the process and even more yes to Him who always says Yes over us. Leaving everything empty before the one who deserves it all. I know this book will be an inspiration and invitation into more of Him.

Lacey Thompson
First Year Director, Bethel School of Supernatural Discipleship

Jenn is a joy to be around and her personality comes out beautifully in her writing. *The War on Your Voice* outlines how process can help lead you to lead a victorious lifestyle in the midst of working through your stuff. Jenn is coming through with flying colors and this book will inspire you to face that process head on.

Marty Pronovost
Senior Leader, Lifehouse Humboldt

I've gotten to know Jenn over the past few years at Bethel Atlanta. Her preached words have always touched a deep and familiar place in my heart. That's why it was a huge honor to edit her written words, but I didn't know it would be so hard to do!

I could hardly focus. Instead of dotting her "i's" and crossing her "t's," I got deeply drawn into her life story and the battle for her voice and identity in Christ. I'd try to edit, but as I read Jenn's words, the Holy Spirit began speaking to the depths of my heart, leading me to introspection and deeper intimacy. The editing process kept turning into an encounter with the Father's heart. Give yourself to Jenn's journey so you can go on your own. Her vulnerability and authenticity are life-giving.

Sherri Lewis, MD
Director of Bethel Atlanta Africa
Author of *The God Zone* and *Effectual: Prayer that Actually Works*

My favorite storytellers let me inside their world, vulnerably share their intimacy with the Father, and reveal the way the Word is shaping their hearts and minds. Jennifer Stockman is just that type of author. These past five years I've come to know her as an absolute delight and a beautiful reflection of our good, good Father. She's a daughter of Light and a carrier of His presence. Often when she preaches, our entire community leans in and smiles. *The War on Your Voice* invites you to join the Apostle Paul in his challenge, 'Imitate me as I imitate Christ.'

Steve Hale
Senior Leader, Bethel Atlanta

Jenn's joyful approach to life, constant pursuit of growth, and intimacy with the Father are contagious. The pages of this book and her heart in it are a beautiful invitation from the Father into an intimate life of love. Her authenticity, vulnerable stories, and personal breakthrough pave a way for others to experience this impartation.

Lauren Brownlee
Senior Leader, Bethel Atlanta

In all the time I have known Jenn, I have been both challenged and inspired by the indelible nature of her love for the Lord. Her trust in Him is absolute, her passion for Him is always growing, and her belief in His goodness is unwavering. She is this person when she is teaching on a stage, she is this person when she is in the office, she is this person when she is with her family and friends, and, unsurprisingly, she is this person in this book.

In reading *The War on Your Voice* you have the opportunity to receive an impartation to step into a level of relationship with the Lord that you may have thought impossible. As you read you will discover that the limits and lies that have been choking your destiny have lost all their strength, and that you are truly significant in the sight of the King of all kings.

Blake K Healy
Director of the Bethel Atlanta School of Supernatural Ministry
Author of *The Veil*

The War On Your Voice

Jenn Stockman

Dedication

To my husband, my hero, my favorite friend. Justin, you have relentlessly taught me that I'm worth fighting for and you are the richest gift I've ever been given.

To my four daughters, my joy, my happiest thought. Kylie, Ava, Arabelle and Liberty, I write and I war with you ever on my mind and closest to my heart.

Acknowledgments

I HAVE BEEN profoundly impacted by the fathers and mothers in the churches the Lord has so graciously placed me in over the years. Thank you, Rio Dell Baptist Church, Bethel Redding, Lifehouse Humboldt and my current home church, Bethel Atlanta. Your relentless and steadfast passion for Jesus has shaped who I am. I am fruit of your generous and bold investment in the Bride of Christ. Thank you for believing she is worth it, pure, spotless and prized. I have become what you have seen through the all-sufficient sacrifice of Jesus and believe, like you, in the bright, shining future of His church.

Thank you to my editor, Sherri Lewis. Your attention and care over my work has left an eternal mark on this manuscript and my heart. Your strength by my side has made me better, so much better.

Thank you to Bethel Atlanta Senior Leadership Team, Steve, Lauren and Blake. Your generous investment in Brett's excellent work on my cover has surrounded my message in your love and support. I'm so grateful!

Foreword

"Fantasy is a dream that never paid a price."

As I first read these words I thought, *Where did Jenn get those from? Where did that fellow, yet a much younger student of Bethel School of Supernatural Ministry find them? The Jenn who was a little unsure of herself, tending to self-doubt and preferring to let others speak instead of her.*

But with those thoughts came the knowledge that they are the fruit of a battle, a war, a price paid. They are the evidence that she is qualified to write what she has written here. She is living a dream, but that dream came with a price which she has willingly paid and now presents to us, the readers, as an invitation to pursue our dreams and leave fantasy, lies, and doubt behind.

Jenn will always be a precious part of my personal story. It was she who first challenged me to learn how to 'father' daughters; this father of sons, who ran male prisons and barely used the word daughter. She told me what I needed to learn to do and offered to be my first project. She is the one who always makes me laugh or smile at anecdotes of those days in BSSM. She demonstrates how much she loves others. She is the one who gathers many around her and lets them know they are deeply loved.

Jenn, you've done it. You've articulated in a way that is completely you, the war which many of us have seen you live and thrive in. A Mom of girls who is determined that every battle of her life will become a victory which "her girls" will inherit.

Jenn's stories are real, raw and beautifully articulated. I hope as a reader who may not know her, that you understand that those of us who do know her, know that the way she has written is indeed who she is. Although there were many stories which I had not been privileged to hear before, I know the woman behind them and I can vouch for her integrity.

I am sure you will find your voice in here. Maybe your victory will come a little easier because Jenn has expressed it for you and invited you to enter in. Or perhaps you will open a small crack in a door as you read and begin your journey of finding your voice and freedom.

Jenn leaves us all believing that we too can dream, that we can be restored to the wholeness which we were created in.

What is the voice which you need to find? The voice which tells the story of your abuse? The voice which is powerful to confront? The voice which motivates those you influence? Perhaps it is the voice of father God you need to find or to give a voice to those who you love the most to speak into your life?

I am confident that you will find keys for your discovery in this beautiful book.

Jenn gifts us with hope and as she said, "Hope is not a fantasy."

Well done Jenn, very well done. Writing forewords is always an honor and a wrestle between a summary of a book and a celebration of the author and what they mean to me. This was not in your case a difficult task. The author and the book are so woven together and so to celebrate the content is to celebrate the author.

One day your girls will read this for themselves. They will celebrate their freedom and tell your grandchildren about their Mom and how she won the war with her voice and gave them theirs.

Paul Manwaring
Author of *Kisses from a Good God* & *What on Earth is Glory?*

Introduction

I WROTE THIS book out on my back porch during the early summer mornings. It was one of the most spiritual experiences of my life. I laughed. I cried. I shook. I felt undone and intoxicated by the nearness of Jesus as I typed and typed.

I told the whole story like a drunk person who's lost every sense of self-awareness and self-restraint. I held nothing back, without a care. I read this great quote in the process, "To gain your own voice, you have to forget about having it heard."[1] I forgot about having it heard and wrote for Him and in Him. I fell in love with the process. The writing became my most intimate worship.

I wrote for Him and now I give it to you. I believe in your voice. Not just the ability to speak words from your mouth, but the uninhibited sound of who and Whose you are through the whole of your story.

I see an army of sons and daughters arising in their authority and bending down low enough in their humility to whisper in the ear of a hurting generation about a relentless, eternal Hope. Jesus loves to live with dirt on His knees and who can resist wanting to be with Him where He is. Humility is telling the real story – nothing more, nothing less.

Shame is terrified that we would live loud the beauty of Christ within us without restraint, naked and unashamed. Every morning when you wake up, your enemy is tormented by the sound of who you are. He's in the corner holding his breath with anxiety, knowing today could be the day you live the truth of Who you belong to. I pray your life gives him a panic attack as you open wide the door to feast with King Jesus, having nothing to hide through the whole of your story.

With all my love,
Jenn

Table of Contents

Chapter I
Up From the Ashes

I SLIPPED OUT of my dorm one weary, college afternoon to head to the prayer room. The little nook had become my favorite corner on the buzzing campus. I was alone and spilling my heart before the Lord. I felt compelled to pray out loud that day instead of my normal habit of quietly processing on the pages of my journal.

As clear as I've ever heard any audible sound, I was jolted from my prayer by a harsh and dark voice. "**Shut the %@#* up!**"

An eerie feeling rushed through my body and my heart shook. Without a thought, I jumped up and raced out of the room with the adrenaline of fear violently pushing behind me. The demonic realm opened up to my physical ear for the first time and some evil spirit was cussing at me to shut up. I was shocked and entirely confused at what had just happened. Of all the things I could think the enemy would want to shout over my life with profanity, "shut up" was definitely not one of them.

If we look back through our history, we see a clearer picture than what we can see up close in a present moment. For years, I'd had a repetitive dream that someone was in terrible danger and I was trying to shout to warn them, but something was suffocating my voice. Different, life-threatening scenario in every dream, but always the same outcome; I was powerless to speak. The dreams were a manifestation of how I truly felt. Feeling like my voice was suffocated wasn't fruit of my personality type or a lack of boldness, but the result of my internal reality. "But what comes out of your mouth reveals the core of your heart" (Matthew 15:18a TPT).

Your voice is infinitely more than just the ability to speak words from your mouth. Your voice begins down in the deep and is the uninhibited sound of who and Whose you are. The whole of your story is speaking about the reality and nature of the One you belong to, *your* Father. Anyone can say something for you, but no one can say something as you. People can tell your story even after you've left the earth, but no one will ever live your story. In your entire lifetime, your story is the only one in which your voice will have the leading role. The devil is terrified that you would fall in love with your story, because loving your story is loving and trusting the One who is writing it.

The devil wasn't cussing at me to shut up because the words I prayed were so powerful. He was terrified that I would soon discover I am eternally and intimately connected to the Person of power, down in the deep of my heart. He can't handle the sound of a child, freely and boldly connecting with her Father. It reminds him of the absolute sufficiency in everything Jesus won and that the uninhibited sound of who you are is the beauty of Jesus on display.

In the Beginning
You didn't begin in your mother's womb or even in Genesis 1. You began in the heart of your God before the foundation of the world.

"And He chose us to be His very own, joining us to Himself even before He laid the foundation of the universe! Because of His great love, He ordained us, so that we would be seen as holy in His eyes with an unstained innocence. For it was always in His perfect plan to adopt us as His delightful children" (Ephesians 1:4-5a TPT).

God wasn't sad, in need, or in a deficit before the story of creation began. "So my Father, restore Me back to the glory that we shared together when we were face-to-face before the universe was created" (John 17:5 TPT).

You began from the fullness of His glory. You weren't needed; you were wanted. From the beginning, your value would never come from what you could offer Him, but who you are to Him. You will never be second-class or one that is less than. You are His. You are the best of your Creator.

He knew sin would come in and twist up our story. Violation after violation of perfect love would confuse our design. Trauma and poor choices would break us beyond repair. He knew we would need to be born again.

> For you know that your lives were ransomed once and for all from the empty futile way of life handed down from generation to generation. It was not a ransom payment of silver and gold, which eventually perishes, but the precious blood of Christ-who like a spotless, unblemished lamb was sacrificed for us. This was part of God's plan, for He was chosen and destined for this before the foundation of the earth was laid.
>
> 1 Peter 1:18-20a TPT

Jesus would finish the brokenness in our story. He was buried, three days in the dark void of the grave and the devil thought He was finished – gone for good. Jesus had His finest hour in the dark. He rose up out of the grave with every demon in hell forever under His victorious, nail-pierced foot. When every demon in hell thinks your voice is buried and gone for good, you, too, will have your finest hour. You will rise up covered head to foot in ashes and soot, with a terrifying whisper, "My story isn't finished yet."

The whole earth is groaning with anticipation, longing to hear the sound of sons, the sound of daughters, who cry, "Abba! Father!" (Romans 8:15,19). Sonship is the sound of a rolled-away stone. Sons and daughters manifest resurrection and relentless hope. They are like the trumpet in Revelation, inviting the weary through the open door of Jesus, "Come up here!" The voice of sonship is the sound of belonging. You belong to the Father.

Fullness of the Time

I will never forget the moment I first realized I was in a war on my voice. I was pregnant with my first baby girl. I was lying awkwardly in bed with my giant belly. Rolling over had become quite the event. I couldn't sleep. My soul was tossing and turning through uncharted territory, just like my overtaken body.

The Father was asking me to have a conversation that felt impossible to have. I would be seeing an extended family member – we'll call him Jim – who I hadn't seen in years. I knew I needed to have a real conversation about a time, years before, when I felt violated and unsafe as a little girl.

I had only known delight and trust in my relationship with Jim until the annual trip "that one summer." He repeatedly cornered me, kissing me in a way that was entirely inappropriate and terrifying on the inside of my little life. I lived as if it never happened with a guarded and distant reservation from that point on.

The little girl in me had grown and matured in healthy identity over the years and the Father was whispering to my spirit, "*You've outgrown the capacity to pretend.*" It's not forgiveness to say nothing and live like it never happened; it's pretending.

I felt powerless and stuck in the deepest part of me and my voice was swallowed up inside my internal reality. I couldn't imagine myself speaking so bold and confident about something so buried and awkward for so many years. It felt impossible.

I argued on the side of shame in my mind, *It's not that big of a deal.*

Freedom argued back, *If it's not that big of a deal, why is there such a wrestle to address it?*

As I tossed and turned, I said, "Father, it feels like You're asking me to get up and run, but I look down and I have no legs."

I believed I had zero capacity to have this type of conversation. I knew it was the healthy and powerful thing to do. For years, I had been deeply impacted by all of Danny Silk's books and messages on living powerful, healthy, and free.[1] I didn't realize the depth of courage it would take to become the message I had fallen in love with. Knowing everything I knew wasn't propelling me forward to do what the Lord was asking me to do. I genuinely felt fine capping out at my current place of growth. If this was as healthy as I would ever be, I felt fine with that. I can love my family well, love Jesus well, and live a quiet life.

As I wrestled there in the dark, the Father spoke. In a moment, His words changed the rest of my life. *"It's okay if you don't want to have the conversation. I will not love you more. I will not love you less. But, if you choose not to face this giant that's chasing you down and taunting you on every side, one day your daughter will lie in a bed just like you. She will feel the same torment of being powerless and stuck inside. She will inherit this giant roaming your land. She will have to choose to face it or run and hide."*

In that one moment, I knew, without a doubt, I would pay any price. I would have any conversation. A face I had yet to see – a little person growing in my womb – was being impacted by my choices. I would give my life to look her in the eye and know I gave my all so this giant wouldn't roam her land and suffocate her voice in the dark of the night.

The War is Real
I was unaware that my feeling so powerless and trapped was because an enemy was pushing me into a corner intending to keep me, my children, and my children's children silent for the rest of time. I was unaware that I was in a war.

David found himself in the middle of a battlefield that day he was bringing his brothers sandwiches. Nine-foot tall Goliath came out morning and night for forty days, taunting the army of God. "When Saul and all Israel heard those words of the Philistine, they were dismayed, and greatly afraid" (1 Samuel 17:11 ESV).

Goliath was intentionally intimidating his enemy with his words. Our enemy, the father of lies, has the same strategy. He only has one weapon and it's talking. There's zero life force in his words unless we agree in fear that what he says could possibly be true. David listened and used the enemy's words to fuel his passion and courage to take action.

When we can actually hear the lie in our mind – the words being shouted morning and night – we are empowered to look the lie in the eyes and courageously speak the truth with the whole of our voice. Goliath was taunting, defying, and mocking David's God.

David looked Goliath straight in the eyes and responded,

> You come to me with a sword and with a spear and with a javelin, but I come to you in the name of the Lord of hosts, the God of the armies of Israel, Whom you have defied. This day the Lord will deliver you into my hand, and I will strike you down and cut off your head that all the earth may know that there is a God in Israel, and that all this assembly may know that the Lord saves not with sword and spear.

> 1 Samuel 17:45-47 ESV

Goliath fell flat because the reality of our God towers over the lie that anything or anyone can tower over His people. Your enemy hates your God and your God hates your enemy.

I had a dream once that a giant, Goliath-like bear was chasing my husband, Justin, and I. We were running for our lives through an overgrown, dark forest. Gasping for air, we fell behind a tree, thinking we were safe enough to catch our breath and take a rest. Before we could halfway slump down, there was the bear, barreling around the corner in terrifying pursuit. We ran and ran. We came upon a little restaurant in the middle of the forest. We darted inside and finally sat down, sure he would never find us in there. At that moment, the bear appeared, mouth watering, arms raised, seeing us completely. My heart dropped in hopeless, exhausted despair. I thought, *There's nowhere to rest and hide from this bear.* Then I woke up.

Fear exhausts us with a race we were never designed to run. Greater is He who is in us than any terrifying bear or giant Goliath we could ever face in this world (1 John 4:4). Fear is an agreement on the inside, so there is truly nowhere to run and hide. However you arrange your life, wherever you go to relieve the pressure of fear, there you are.

We were born for this war. We were designed to stop running, look the lies straight in the eyes, and get close enough to hear the words fear is shouting morning and night. Behind the giant voice of fear is a little lie tormenting us on the inside. When we can hear the lie, we can hear the agenda of fear to steal our land and push us into tiny corners we were never born for.

Jubilee

The tightly shut up walls of Jericho stood between the people of God and the wide-open Promised Land they were born for. A sound would cause the walls to crumble before them. "And when they make a long blast with the ram's horn, when you hear the sound of the trumpet, then all the people shall shout with a great shout, and the wall of the city will fall down flat" (Joshua 6:5 ESV).

The trumpet used was not the standard battle trumpet that called warriors to war. It was the one blown to proclaim the highly anticipated Year of Jubilee, initiating celebration. It is the sound that set bound captives free and took the crushing weight of man's debt and forgave it completely. It was the sound of hope spilling into every low place of despair and brought absolute certainty that the favor of the Lord was near. The kind intention, goodness, and mercy of their God were heard in the trumpet sound. We can imagine the over-whelming response to the trumpet – an eruption of joyful shouts, dancing and tearful cheers.

In Jericho, the people of God were marching for seven days in silence around massive walls, anticipating the sound that would initiate their one job – shout.

Joshua and his army were commissioned to take the land of Jericho, but not with a war cry or incredible military strategy. They would take the land with a sound, the sound of Jubilee and the shouts of celebration.

Jesus had something to say about Jubilee the day He first stepped into the Nazareth synagogue. He opened the scroll of Isaiah and stood up to read His inaugural message.

> "The Spirit of the Lord is upon me, because He has anointed me to proclaim good news to the poor. He has sent me to proclaim liberty to the captives and recovering of sight to the blind, to set at liberty those who are oppressed, to proclaim the year of the Lord's favor." And He rolled up the scroll and gave it back to the attendant and sat down. And the eyes of all in the synagogue were fixed on Him. And He began to say to them, 'Today this scripture has been fulfilled in your hearing.'"

> Luke 4:18-21 ESV

He was pronouncing that He, Himself, is the favorable year of the Lord. He is the Person of Jubilee. He is our freedom, hope and healing. The wait is over.

Jesus commissioned His disciples, " 'As the Father has sent me, even so I am sending you.' And when He had said this, He breathed on them and said to them, 'Receive the Holy Spirit. If you forgive the sins of any, they are forgiven them, if you withhold forgiveness from any, it is withheld' " (John 20:21-23 ESV).

He blew on them as an instrument in the hand of Lord to receive the same Spirit that was upon Him. That same Holy Spirit would blow through them the sound of Jesus. The sound of debts forgiven, everlasting freedom and the Lord's favor setting every captive eternally free.

From generation to generation, this sound of our Savior is to fill the whole earth, cause every wall to fall flat, every knee to bow and every dead thing to arise in resurrected life. Sons and daughters live inside a triumphant, joyful shout.

We are not shouting because we are in a war to be set free. Paul and Silas manifested this truth in Acts 16 when they were thrown into prison and bound with shackles around their feet. They began to lift their voice in song and an earthquake opened every door and unfastened every shackle. If they were singing to be set free, they would have ran straight through the open door rejoicing but they didn't. They remained in the prison.

They sang because they were already free. Bondage wants us to believe freedom will always be just out of reach. *Shout louder and sing longer so you can finally be free. You're a captive waiting for release.* Bondage is a liar. The Gospel is the good news that Jesus came and gifted us freedom that reaches down to the most bound up places in our soul, for free. Our war is with any lie muzzling the true sound of our freedom in Christ.

Breakthrough

We are designed to break through the lies bondage whispers in prison cells and the lies giants of fear scream to keep us out of the land we were born for. I can't help but think of a little chick every time I feel the invitation for breakthrough swelling up within me. Every day, a mama hen cares for her little chick by flipping the egg and warming it with her presence. Flip, warm, repeat, until about the seventeenth day.

Her chick begins to make noises and the mama hen becomes more attentive to her little egg. She knows its time of development no longer needs the warmth of her presence, but watchful nearness as the little chick works hard to break through.

An egg tooth develops out of the chick's beak for the sole purpose of piercing through the shell. It can take days of diligent work. The mama hen wouldn't dare help from the outside. She is entirely aware that muscles to survive on the outside won't grow without the tension inside. The wrestle to break through is the strength that will sustain life on the other side.

Once the chick breaks into the open air, it can walk, see, and eat entirely independent of the mama hen. What a wild moment for the baby chick to experience that those little legs, that tiny beak, and the fluffy, feather wings were all meant for so much more than life in the egg could ever provide.

We often aren't aware of our need for breakthrough until around the "seventeenth day," when the comfort we've always known is suddenly no longer there. It is a lie that our Father has left us stranded on the outside. He is actually more attentive and aware of our development than we ever are. When life begins to feel tight and pressure is closing in on every side, we are being invited into breakthrough. It is a tragedy when we blame our circumstance, or we blame the people "out there" for what's happening on our insides.

The chick doesn't waste strength grumbling that the hen didn't give it a big enough egg to grow and thrive. Thinking a person or a circumstance is responsible for the uncomfortably tight pressure we feel on the inside is a powerless mindset. The chick somehow knows, *I have a tooth. I must have enough to break outside. There must be more than my little egg life.*

Waiting for breakthrough inside the shell when the chick has an egg tooth is a waste of time. The chick doesn't just try. It knows it can't survive any longer inside. It has no option but to break through.

The Father knows your design. You have a voice and it's not to be locked up and suffocated inside a shell. You have a courageous spirit. You have a fearless nature. You are designed to live powerful and free. Like a little chick that discovers it is created for life outside the shell, we discover the fullness of what we were born for on the other side of the wrestle to break through.

He put everything you need in your new nature, ever abiding in Jesus, to break through whatever is binding you up on the inside. He loves you too much to do it for you. It is His belief in us that watches with anticipation and excitement, ever by our side. He sees the tension, the wrestle, the growing muscles in us that are necessary for sustaining the powerful life of freedom that is our portion inside of Christ.

I Believe in You

One night, I saw so clearly the kind intention of the Father on that uncomfortable "seventeenth day." I was tucking in one of my girls at bedtime and she began to cry. I could handle the days when that cry came from a skinned knee or a revolt against bedtime. When it started coming from a deep and real heart pain, I thought that if it didn't kill her, it would definitely kill me.

Two of her dearest friends were moving far away and she was still deeply missing friends and family that were no longer in her daily life because of our recent cross-country move. I was listening and thinking.

Is she going to be okay? I know this pain; it's terrible. Can she handle this much transition? Is there a bubble or egg-shell I can put her in? Will she recover?

I tried to pray something wise, hugged and kissed her then headed out the door.

As I walked away from her room, I heard the sound of my favorite voice – the voice of the Father that always brings hope and gives my life its shape. His voice has zero fear or worry – just perfect love.

He said, *"I believe in her ability to process pain. Do you?"*

In one moment, all the questions bowed to relentless faith. *She is not fragile. She is mighty. She is tender. Her God is alive. Nothing is impossible for her. She is not a victim. She is wired to overcome. I believe in her!*

11

Living with love and honor is living with a belief in our capacity to break through. We learn to believe in ourselves because our Father believes in us. He smiles over our development without interrupting it until we believe what He believes. It's our belief in ourselves and others that actually lifts lids, tears down limitations, and calls us higher. Our life becomes a message, "If I was designed to break through, surely, you too are designed to break through."

We are not victims, held captive by a shell. We are the ones the Father believes in – the ones destined to overcome. One of the most honoring expressions of love we can manifest in our relationships is the message of hope that stands beside development without swooping in to rescue people from their shell. I am not helping when I reinforce the lie of powerlessness within myself or others.

You have authority in your voice. It is like the egg tooth given to break out of the shell. You have a "yes." You have a "no." You have a destiny and a purpose. You have a strength that you and the world needs to know.

If you've tried one hundred times, try one hundred and one. Think a new thought. Tell the truth. Take the risk. Look ridiculous. Feel painfully awkward. Just stay in the wrestle. Just don't give up. There is only one way out of that shell and the most loving eyes of your Father are steady on you.

The Rest of the Story
One of the most significant personal moments I've had of wrestling out of an uncomfortably tight shell and watching walls fall flat came when I traveled out of town with my pregnant belly and saw Jim. I knew my only option was to have that awkward conversation.

We had been visiting family for several days. I waited until the very last moment to talk with him. Knowing I was in a war that impacted my legacy, my daughter's voice and her daughter's voice didn't take away the fear and trembling I felt inside. The dreadful thought of getting in the car suffocated by the regret of not boldly telling the truth became greater than my fear of attempting to speak with a suffocated voice.

I asked Jim to step into a private room. My hero husband came with me like that silent strength of the hen on the "seventeenth day," watching with anticipation, right by my side.

I reached into the dark archive of my story and pulled the whole truth into the light. Our grace and forgiveness for people who hurt us can only go as deep as the truth we share. If we make light of the true trauma – of the real pain and hurt they caused us – then we make light of the true depth in our forgiveness. Jesus came full of grace *and* truth (John 1:14). We must, too.

I started by reminding him of the summer all those years ago where he repeatedly cornered and inappropriately kissed me. I listened as terribly awkward words poured out of my mouth so beautiful, bold and confident. I was absolutely running with the legs the Father always knew I had; that He designed me to have.

I kept going. "I was deeply affected and hurt by what you chose to do. I wanted tell you, I forgive you entirely. I release you. When you look back on your life, I want you to see me with no regret. I want you to feel peace and that all is right when you think of me. I love you. I honor and bless your place in my life."

The inaugural message of Jesus became the inaugural message of my life. I wrapped my arms around this old, weathered man as he sobbed. We were both set free. The sound of Jubilee, the song of Jesus, the Gospel of mercy was enough for me and it was enough for Jim.

I got in the car to leave and sat in a victory I had never known before. I was born for this war and there was victorious blood on my sword. I will never shut up. A thousand pounds of chains had fallen off my life. I felt like the bouncy little chick, wobbling around in newborn joy. The green grass! The fresh air! The beauty of Jesus! Abba! Father!

I looked over at my husband. He was beaming with pride. Confrontation, telling the truth, and having no secrets to hide have always been among his many strengths. What a gift that he never once suggested that he be the one to have the conversation with Jim for me. He believed in me.

I looked down at my baby growing inside. I rested my hand on that giant belly and felt the heart of two warriors growing simultaneously. I lifted my eyes to the uncharted land I knew was mine – rich and bright. I whispered in the light, "My story isn't finished yet."

To live *your* story with *your* voice is to live with a deep value for process.

Chapter 2
The Story of Process

THERE I WAS, a tiny seed so safe in the giant palm of the Farmer's hand. I look up. He smiles. There's a thousand words of love in one blink of His eye. I'm just a little seed that hasn't done a thing, yet He is so pleased. I am His. I feel Him plunge me deep down into the ground. All I can see is darkness and dirt on every side. It smells like manure. My heart starts to panic. The Farmer just buried me alive! I can't see or breathe. I look up under piles of dirt to see if He feels just like me.

He doesn't. He's still happy, smiling wide. I feel worried that the dirt will take root and become me. He's not. Every day, He walks my way and doesn't seem to see the dirt or manure. He just sees me, a tiny seed, growing slow and just right. He bends down and pours water. He thanks the dirt for giving me what I need, for I am His much-loved tree.

I look nothing like a tree, but I feel peace well up inside. The dirt will help me grow. I'm extracting nutrients from the manure down in the deep of my life. In the darkness, I come alive. Creatures walk by and step on me. The earth shakes. I decide not to mind. I learn the Farmer always knows just where I am.

Soon, I sprout up. I grow a trunk, limbs and leaves. Fruit begins to grow all over. The creatures walk by and see me, the abundant and beautiful tree. They love the fruit falling from my limbs. The Farmer leans back in the shade of my leaves. He takes a bite of fruit that grew on His tree. He's so pleased. He tips his head back and laughs. Fruit starts to grow abundant and heavy.

In the cool of the day, the Farmer is coming my way. I see scissors in the palm of His hand. The palm where I began and first learned that only good things come from His hand.

He got close and whispered in my ear, *"You are Mine"* and then clipped my branch. Good, beautiful fruit crashed to the ground. He snipped and snipped until I was naked and bare.

Creatures walked by and whispered, "What a terrible waste."

I lift my eyes and His face makes me forget the fruit I missed. Every season something changes, except that look in His eye.

The best thing about being a tree isn't what I learn in the dirt, the beautiful fruit, or the scissors coming my way. The best thing about being a tree is knowing this Farmer who is ever caring for me.

You belong to this Farmer, the Father. Your voice – the uninhibited sound of who and Whose you are – is not shouting louder in certain seasons than others. The war is on our awareness of that look in His eye that never changes. You are entirely His, down in the dark dirt as a tiny seed and up in the bright light with abundant fruit. The most powerful part of your story will never be found in one extraordinary season, but in the eternal relationship Jesus won to live as the apple of His eye, every moment of every day.

Process

Nothing shouts process quite like a little seed. I was mopping the floor one afternoon and heard the Father ask me a question. *"Would you like to know a synonym for process?"*

I'm a homeschool mom, so He was speaking my language. My first response to the grammar test was, "PAIN!"

He laughed, *"Relationship is a synonym for process."*

"Oh." I laughed.

I began to meditate on the truth of it as I watched sticky floors become shiny again. When we hate the process, we are unknowingly wishing for a religion of rules and legalism with a distant God. Despising the process is wanting a formula that guarantees our desired outcome. A life of grace is a life that gifts us with His Presence. Rules no longer fix our problems. Formulas don't solve our issues.

Emmanuel – God with us – won't rescue us from walking through all the twists and turns of life. He will empower us to walk through it beside Him. He won't be removed and distant as we beg for what we need. We will walk and talk in the cool of the day as we process through life. He won't hand us answers. His Presence will be our answer.

One of my most favorite teachers, Graham Cooke, talks often about how every situation in life is never first about the situation.[1] It is always about an upgrade in our relationship with Jesus. The situation is to lead us to know Him in a way we have never known Him before. When we become over-whelmed by the process, it's an invitation to step deeper into relationship.

I remember being single, driving in my car, in the thick of an incredibly pain-ful process. I was desperate for rescue. The Father asked me, *"Will you give Me time?"*

I wanted a quick fix. He wanted time. I wanted a pill to instantaneously take away all the symptoms. He wanted to grow something deep and rich in the soil of my soul. The more I get to know Him, the more I see He is never in a hurry. Love is never in a hurry. Love is patient. He is eternal. One day is as a thousand years and a thousand years as one day (2 Peter 3:8 ESV). He never feels behind or deficient in time.

I imagine the disciples had to adjust to the nature of Jesus again and again. Surely the Savior of the whole world didn't have time to sit with children.

Surely he was too busy to stop, again. Eternal life is not about getting things done or a race to finish an assignment. Eternal life is about knowing Him (John 17:3). Knowing Him will never be a race and will never have a finish line.

If my dependent little girls woke up and were suddenly sixteen or twenty-two, I would be devastated. I don't want them to stay small forever, but it's definitely the delight of my life to be present and intimately involved as they grow the rest of their lives. I'm not waiting for them to "arrive" at some magical place in their process so I can finally enjoy them.

I could say with confidence at twenty years old that I knew the man I was marrying. Now, fifteen years later of holding hands through twists and turns, dark nights, and bright lights, I *know* my husband.

There's no race in being married or being a parent. We're in it forever. Process becomes rich when our goal is not to finish, but to grow down deep in intimate love and eternal relationship. The sound of our voice bears eternal fruit in every season of our process when we live from relationship with Him. Without this love, our lives become the hollow sound of a clanging cymbal (1 Corinthians 13:1).

"So step into life-union with Me, for I have stepped into life-union with you. For as a branch severed from the vine will not bear fruit, so your life will be fruitless unless you live your life intimately joined to Mine" (John 15:4 TPT).

Ezekiel and Those Bones
Ezekiel 37 speaks so much about the heart of God for process. I remember being nineteen and falling in love with the passage. I read it every morning for months. It became home to me.

It starts with the hand of the Lord reaching out to Ezekiel and walking him down to a valley full of bones. He didn't just point to them, but walked him around and through them. There were many and they were very dry. The valley was a battleground and the bones were piled high because the people of God didn't leave alive. The Lord was walking through the places of hopeless despair. Bodies died. Hearts died. Dreams died. The Lord invited Ezekiel on a walk and headed straight into piles of defeat.

The Lord breaks the somber silence by asking Ezekiel, *"Can these bones live again?"*

The bones were very dry. You couldn't make out a person or call out a name. There wasn't a sliver of hope in that valley. The obvious answer is, "**NO**, they cannot Lord."

But, Ezekiel is wise, and says, "You alone know, Lord."

If we don't know the heart of God, it can feel cruel when He leads us to these places of death and defeat. It's a terribly painful place to pick for a walk. He intentionally leads us to the places where something in us died because His heart is always for resurrection and life.

I will never forget the night the Lord grabbed me by the hand and walked me into a valley of dry bones. It was a Monday night at Bethel Atlanta School of Supernatural Ministry (BASSM). It was my first year in a director role and I was laid out with my face buried in the carpet and a puddle of tears. For a second I wondered, *Is this ok?*

Before I could finish the question, I knew I never wanted to lead from anywhere but right there. The Lord grabbed my hand and was walking me through memories that had been buried in a dead valley for years.

I was little, cheery and bright. I was sitting on the lap of my uncle who stole my heart. He was so big, with dark skin and looked just like an Indian. He had tattoos all up his arms and wore oxygen in his nose. He kept my photo right by his chair and I always felt loved and especially adored there on his lap. We ate strawberry waffles for breakfast in between sessions of me "removing his tattoos." I didn't know much of his story or his life. I just knew he loved me.

The Lord walked me around and about, passing by what had died. I was sexually abused by someone else there in my uncle's house. Feeling so safe and the deep delight of being the apple of my uncle's eye, died. I put him and all the memories out of my mind. My unconscious response to the abuse was to forget *all* of it, not just the traumatic stuff.

As I grew, he would question where I was. I never stopped by to explain what had happened and tell him how much I loved him. It wasn't even an option in my thinking as a young girl who hadn't begun to process the pain and trauma from the abuse.

In my adult life, I heard the news that he took his life. I never said goodbye. I never explained a thing. The guilt and shame surrounded my memory of him.

I had received so much healing from the sexual abuse through the years, but on this night at BASSM, the Lord was pointing to a love that had died. I sobbed as I felt His heart care for what I was fine to leave in the valley as a lost battle until heaven restored it on the other side. The heart of Jesus was grieved at what was lost. It was still on His mind. He wanted to take a walk and remind me where there once was life, because He was there and hated watching it die.

I can imagine the look in the Lord's eye when He asked Ezekiel if the bones could live again. "We both know they couldn't be more dead, right Zeke?" Winking with kindness in His eyes – "Watch this, son."

The Lord could have said in a moment, "Rise up and come to life," and that entire valley would've stood on its feet. His voice spoke the whole world into existence out of nothing. The Lord wanted to co-labor with Ezekiel from their relationship and hear the sound of his voice by His side. God valued Ezekiel's voice in the process. He told Ezekiel to prophesy and wanted him to speak to every little thing that had died.

To the bones, "I saw you die. Come to life." The skin, "I saw you die. Come to life." The breath. "I saw you die. Come to life."

He heard them rattle and shake and burst forth into life. It was an army of hope standing in resurrected life! The passage is a prophetic picture of a Savior who would come to call hopelessly dead things back to life. Jesus came walking in and through every valley. "I am the resurrection and the life" (John 11:25 ESV).

Weeks after that night buried in the carpet at BASSM, I was at the Atlanta Zoo with my family. We were still transitioning from the brisk fog of the Northern California Coast to the southern life of hot, Georgia humidity. Justin and the big girls were playing on the slides and I was nursing a sweaty baby on a bench outside. I looked over and saw a large, Indian man, with tattoos and an oxygen tank walking my way. My heart began to race as I instantly thought of my uncle who looked incredibly similar to this man. I felt the nearness of heaven being at hand as this man sat by my side.

He was a complete stranger, but began asking me about my life with such ease like we had known each other forever. We talked about cross-country transition and how good it would be for my family and life. He told me what a good thing it was that I would nurse my baby. I felt so comforted by his words and my body was a little shaky the entire time, knowing I was in a supernaturally ordained moment. My family came from the playground and I introduced them to this beautiful, Indian man. We got up to leave and this stranger sent from Jesus looked me straight in the eye and said, "I'm proud of you."

I walked away, melted inside. The guilt and shame of cutting my uncle out of my life without ever saying goodbye was swallowed up and overcome in a moment. For the first time, I could think of my uncle in heaven with the cloud of witnesses, proud of me. Jesus was calling dead things back to life. He was restoring the heart of a girl who wouldn't have to run or hide when deep springs of love opened up in my life. It's safe to be special and the apple of His eye. If your voice isn't drenched in the sound of redemption, overwhelming restoration, and a fresh well of love, the story of Jesus isn't finished yet.

The Seed

Jesus has a way of turning piles of defeat into hope-filled armies. When He asks for time, it's because He's growing something authentic and deep. He never orchestrates the death or defeat, but He uses it brilliantly as the dirt for a seed.

Psalm 84:5-7 says,

How enriched are they who find their strength in the Lord, within their hearts are the highways of holiness! Even when their path winds through the dark valley of tears, they dig deep to find a pleasant pool where others find only pain. He gives to them a brook of blessing filled from the rain of an outpouring. They grow stronger and stronger with every step forward, until they find all their strength in you (TPT).

Under the pain and dark valley of tears, there is a deep well of outpouring. It's a process to dig deeper than pain's surface. For so long, I hated pain and was constantly desperate for rescue from its grip on my life.

One Sunday morning, I was in worship and I felt the place of pain in my heart surface that I had been fiercely despising and wishing away, whatever the cost. I saw Jesus point to that place and say, *"I have my eye on **her**."* I didn't realize hating the pain was hating a place in my heart. He was letting me know, He would never just throw her out. He intended to set me free, but not on the surface – down in the deep.

I was tormented with loneliness for years of my life. I've always been surrounded by beautiful people, but this place of loneliness was a growing ache in my heart. My first year of marriage was one of the loneliest because I thought for sure a husband would end the painful wrestle. I always felt like a lost visitor that stumbled into a terribly ravished, barren, dark land. I was never sure how I got stuck there and felt powerless to stumble back out.

Everything changed when I realized this was actually *my* land. I wasn't a visitor at all. I was the owner of this lonely, painful land. A part of my heart was lonely, and it didn't help that I kept wishing her away. I felt the invitation of Jesus to turn this into our favorite place to walk, talk, sip some coffee – live in intimacy.

Psalm 126: 5-6 says, "Those who sow their tears as seeds, will reap a harvest with joyful shouts of glee. They may weep as they go out carrying their seed to sow, but they will return with joyful laughter, and shouting with gladness as they bring back armloads of blessing, and a harvest overflowing!" (TPT)

We sow in tears when it's a dry and barren land that hasn't been yielding any fruit. We are hungry and in lack as we put the seeds in the ground. It's not instant provision or instant fulfillment. It's a process of tender care as the seeds are nourished into life-giving growth.

When I felt painfully lonely, instead of rejecting that land, I would go sit close to that part of my heart. I would put love in the ground. You're worth loving when you're lonely. You're worth having a voice when your land feels barren. What a tragedy when we're busy hugging the whole world whole and our own heart feels like a rejected, barren land.

I would whisper to that part of my heart, "You have time. No matter how long you feel lonely, I'll be here."

I would put patience in the ground. I wouldn't leave the place of loneliness to find my voice of worship. I would lift my voice in worship from the place of loneliness. Intimacy is coming just as I am. I would sow that as seeds into the ground.

I fell in love with every inch of that land. I fell in love with the patience of Jesus who was never in a hurry to race away to a prettier place. He had His eye ever on this barren place inside of me. That part of my heart didn't become beautiful because the loneliness was loved away. She realized she had always been beautiful because Jesus loved her just the same – lonely, barren, fruitful, or free. I couldn't help but want to be just like Him.

Down in the Deep

No amount of human affection could fill up the void in our soul. If the whole world shouted your name, fiercely loved and adored you, you could still feel lonely inside. If the whole world hated you, rejected you and slandered your name, you could still feel full and abundant inside. We aren't wired to live from the outside in. We are wired to live from the inside out.

Jesus, on the brink of being crucified, said to His closest friends, "You will be scattered, each to his own home, and will leave me alone. Yet I am not alone, for the Father is with me" (John 16:32 ESV).

Jesus felt connected and full of the nearness of His Father in the face of real abandonment and rejection. He came to show us the eternal reality of an ever-present Father. He's present for deep, intimate connection – to provide and protect in every season of our process. We can always say like Jesus, "He is with me."

When we live looking to our outside world to fix what's happening within, it's never enough. Jesus was constantly giving the Pharisees feedback about their long robes, their need for the best seat, their special greetings and showy prayers to impress everyone around. They were trying to arrange their outside world to fill up the void in their soul. They wanted to feel important, significant and uniquely valuable. They couldn't go to the bottom of the void and see, outside affirmation would never be enough.

Believing that something on the outside can fix the void on the inside is a trick to bind us up with lack. They needed a Savior. Without Him, everything coming from the outside runs out like a hole in a broken bucket of the soul. We needed an eternal, unconditional Love that would never run dry.

"On the last day of the feast, the great day, Jesus stood up and cried out, 'If anyone thirsts, let him come to me and drink. Whoever believes in Me, as the Scripture has said, 'Out of his heart will flow rivers of living water'" (John 7:37-38 ESV).

There's only one place to quench our thirst to feel important, significant and uniquely valuable. Believe in Him. Feel rejection and believe in His love. Feel alone and believe in His nearness. His Spirit inside is filling every thirsty place like rushing rivers so full, they have to spill over to the outside.

In Christ, we are not broken people trying to get whole. We are not unhealthy people struggling to get free. Healthy and whole is how we start as born-again believers in Jesus. We are the healthy seed using the overwhelming dirt of life to help us grow strong and true. Nothing can contaminate what Jesus made clean. We are a new creation, growing up in the gift of a righteous blood-line. Healthy kids grow. Healthy trees grow. Healthy people keep growing in health.

Newly married, I threw myself into counseling for a year. My life revolved around not missing a session. I felt twisted up and wrong inside and was determined and so desperate to live free. Someone told me, "It's interesting that you married Justin. Normally, unhealthy people marry unhealthy people. But you married a healthy person."

I had so much faith in my unhealthy nature that I completely agreed. Trying so hard to get healthy was a dead-end street. At the end of the year, Jesus came with a question. *"Are you pursuing health or are you pursuing Me?"*

Our old nature with our old voice was broken beyond repair. We were unhealthy and twisted in shame far beyond what any help could ever restore.

We could chase health our entire lives and still it wouldn't be enough. Jesus took our unhealthy, twisted up nature as His own. He was our only hope to ever live whole. He hung lifeless, broken beyond repair, crushing death's despair once and for all. He purchased and bought every twisted thing in your soul. It no longer belongs to you. In exchange, He handed you His perfect life, His perfect voice.

You are a healthy person learning to live whole. It's so important to know where we start or we could spend our entire life working to become something we already are. I absolutely believe in Christian counseling and inner healing resources when it's a tool to help healthy people grow. I have been tremendously helped by it. I have needed and still need a ton of help, learning to live healthy and whole, but I no longer strive to become it. I was born again, healthy and whole, and I process through growth from there, not in search of it.

There is a war to bury your voice, the truest sound of who and Whose you are, under the lie that wholeness will always be that dangling carrot just out of reach. Jesus won us a new identity that is no longer defined by the limp of our brokenness. The feet of sons and daughters have been made strong to walk **through** pain and process, growing up into the nature of our perfect Father. Healthy kids take time to grow into the fullness of who they are and at the very heart of your new identity is childlike sonship.

Living in Christlikeness is living in sonship. Jesus is known as the Son of God for all of eternity. Because of Him, wherever you are in your growth, however slow it feels, you will never be more or less of His child for all of eternity.

You have been set free from every lid on your capacity to grow into His likeness. Today, in the thick of your process, your enemy is terrified at the sound of your voice living loud on the earth because it shouts of a wholeness that isn't a destination out in *someday,* but a gift found only in Jesus.

Fruitfulness

Jesus cares more about the health of our voice than the amount of fruit it can produce. Seasons of pruning remind us of this beautiful truth. Right after I got back from the weekend of feeling freed from the muzzle on my voice that we talked about in the previous chapter, my pastor asked me to speak on a Sunday night for the very first time. He saw something in me I didn't see.

I was so nervous. I wrote really detailed notes. My voice was shaking and I felt like I couldn't breathe. As I got going, my mind cleared and I felt myself releasing keys that were setting people free. I started getting more opportunities to speak and realized there is a teaching gift on my life. I got in a good groove of writing out everything ahead of time and clinging to my notes. Seeing those notes would remind my anxious mind of what I wanted to say when I felt overwhelmed by the nerves.

I will never forget the Sunday morning I was sitting in service at Lifehouse Fortuna, waiting to speak. I quietly but surely heard the Holy Spirit say, *"Leave your notes."*

He was inviting me to trust Him. I gave a heart racing "yes" and felt another layer of the fear of man being burnt off my life. I stepped into something so beautiful that day. As soon as I finished a thought, I saw in my mind the next thing He wanted me to say. He was giving me permission to keep my eyes steady and dependent on Him. I felt myself bearing more fruit.

Over time, I felt the fruit start to get heavy inside. It seeped into my identity and I started to feel pressure to produce. I loved the moments when I would speak, but I started despising the moments leading up to it and after I was done. Feeling stuck, I began telling the Lord, "I just want to work at Kmart."

The gifts that are meant to give life and nourishment to the world around us will end up crushing the life and nourishment right out of us if we believe those gifts give us our value and define us. I'll talk more about that in chapter four. A season of scissors – of pruning – was coming my way.

I got help from a friend, Chuck. He'd weathered many years of ministry life and was still so light and in love. He told me I had a boundary problem.

Before I would speak, my heart was screaming, "I don't want to do this!" Instead of working so hard to silence the voice of my heart, I needed to respond and listen. Saying no to opportunities to speak, setting a personal boundary, would give the lies perpetuating the cycle an opportunity to rise to the surface. I could then process and get to the root of the problem.

"Up and out," Chuck said.

That was Thursday. On Sunday, I was scheduled to speak at a friend's church. I called and said "no." I waited and felt nothing until Sunday morning, at the time I was supposed to speak. The lies and feelings came crashing in like a flood. I felt like a failure and felt a drop in my worth. The thoughts that were perpetuating the cycle had a chance to come "up and out" so they could be brought before the Father. He drew close and snipped and snipped.

In the same season, I remember sitting with the Lord one afternoon, feeling naked and awkward without the fruit covering up most of me.

He said, *"I'm not using you."*

I listened, confused. I had prayed that prayer, "Use me, Lord," for years of my life.

He kept going, *"I have no end goal in mind for your life. I'm not trying to fix you up so I can finally do something productive with you."*

He is my Father. Not a boss, coach, or production manager. He's the One I come from. I am His. He wants to know me – *to know me*. He wants to love me – *to love me*. He wants to be near to me – *to be near to me*.

We are designed to bear ever increasing, supernatural fruit. The kind that can't come from striving or a pressure to produce. The kind that only grows from a promise if we rest and abide.

In the book of Numbers, Joshua and Caleb brought a cluster of grapes from the Promised Land that was so big, it had to be carried on a pole between two men (Numbers 13:23). The goal was never for men to be impressed by the fruit and honor it as the prize of their life. They weren't to hang it on the wall and celebrate a land they once saw. The crazy fruit was to draw them into passion to take the land.

The land of our Promise is the land of intimacy. The constant Presence of the Father, Son and Holy Spirit – no matter the season, no matter the process of the tree. Seasons change with times of sowing, reaping, and pruning, but every season is a season of intimacy. When the earth shakes and we shake too, it's good to let the seed seep down into the deep where intimacy is rich and pure.

We are constantly growing our intimacy to be bigger and wider than anything growing on the outside. When opportunities or relationships or work cause us to lose our peace and our world begins to shake, it's time to grow a life of intimacy that can absorb the uncertainty in process.

Jesus lived in such a way that nothing was ever bigger than His peace with the Father. When ministry no longer feels light and full of love, it's time to go home to Him and grow an intimate life that's bigger than what we have to give. When a relationship feels rocky and it's stealing our place of rest, it's time to upgrade all our rest into this Jesus who slept through the storm in the cabin of the ship (Mark 4:38).

Now whenever I teach, I treasure the moments before and the moments after as much as what happens in between. Nothing means more to me or could ever be greater than the rest in being His.

Walk with Him

Process doesn't define who you'll be in your relationship with Him. Your relationship with Him defines who you will be in the process. The Holy Spirit came upon Jesus and led Him on purpose into the wilderness (Luke 4:1).

He took Him on a walk in an undesirable land. He walked Him into a process. He didn't eat food or drink water. The devil himself came and questioned Him, the last person anyone wants to talk to – no matter where you are. The wilderness was famous for being the place the people of God were punished to wander for forty years. The Father had just publicly affirmed, *"This is my beloved Son in whom I am well pleased"* (Matthew 3:17 ESV).

The pleasure of the Father and the Presence of the Holy Spirit walked Him into the wilderness. It's a place of punishment no longer. Our external circumstance is not punishment. The process of our life is not punishment from our Father.

Jesus was in the wilderness. The Eternal Well of Living Water was in a barren land. The Prince of Peace and God of all Hope was standing in an isolated land for forty days.

None of the nature of Jesus was restricted in the wilderness. If you are in the wilderness and there's no one but the devil to talk to, Jesus has been there. None of His nature is restricted in you.

The wilderness is a place where your identity in Christ has space to come fully alive. There's no place too dry, there's no process too deep for the promise of Jesus to reach out His hand and walk with you in that land.

Jesus returned from the wilderness in the power of the Holy Spirit. He left leaning and empowered. Song of Solomon 8:5 says, "Who is that coming up from the wilderness, leaning on her beloved?" (ESV).

Leave the wilderness leaning on your Beloved. Don't leave with a limp of offense or hanging your head in weary despair. Lean because you tasted a Person of power who set your voice wildly free to speak of Whose you are in every season, circumstance and process. Lean because you became too intoxicated, too undone in love with your Beloved, to walk any longer on your own.

It's in the leaning that we learn to live healthy and whole, without shame. We are the ones walking through every process and coming up from every wilderness with an unreserved, uninhibited voice that's entirely free from the lids of shame that lie in the dark.

Chapter 3
Shame is a Liar in the Dark

I WAS SITTING in my first sozo (a beautiful inner healing ministry) as a first year Bethel School of Supernatural Ministry student in Redding, California. I was doing my best to pry open my troubled soul to complete strangers sitting across from me. My search for honest answers to their questions was like fingertips racing along a textured wall in a dark room, desperate for a light switch.

I suddenly stumbled headfirst into a memory. I sat there so still, but inside my world was spinning. Waves of nausea started spilling through my body until I was on the verge of throwing up. I don't remember the questions asked or the doors that were opened, but somehow we landed there.

I was about six years old, hiding in the back alley behind a house. The neighbor boy and me had been hiding and sneaking, having oral sex regularly. This particular day, we were there in the narrow alley. I felt big and in control until someone suddenly jumped on the fence. My fake fortress of safety came crashing down as a violent fear of being exposed turned my world green with nausea. Shame was there that day calling me into the darkness, into hiding, to give me a name. You are dirty. You are wrong. You are dark.

When you're six, you feel big. You feel responsible. You feel the name shame gave you in the dark alley is true and right and deserved. It takes time to grow big enough to see how little six is. I sat in that chair as a grown adult, but my heart was stuck, suffocating under a pile of fig leaves as a six year-old.

Dr. Henry Cloud in his book, *Changes that Heal,* calls this bad time passing. Healing and growing both take time. When a trauma or significant life event takes place and we don't have what we need to grow and process through it, time keeps passing, but we are stuck. We're viewing life through a stunted lens. When we're stuck, our voice is stuck.

Father Shame

Shame keeps our voice stuck under a lid. The spirit of shame intends to father us and silence the truest sound of who and Whose we are for the rest of our lives. The war is not to defeat the power of shame; Jesus finished that. The war is over our awareness of who our true Father is. Winning the war is refusing to respond to the names shame gave us in dark alleys.

Fathers give us a name and call us by it the whole of our life, reinforcing the reality of our identity. When King Nebuchadnezzar besieged Jerusalem and took for himself youth from the royal family and nobility, the first thing he did was change the boys' names (Daniel 1). If he had their identity, he had their voice. Their gifts, talents and potential would be at his disposal to advance his agenda and kingdom.

The youth from the royal family were the hope of Israel's future, the seed of the kingdom. These boys were between thirteen and twenty years old and had just endured the defeat of their people and their God. Along with them, Nebuchadnezzar took some of the vessels of the house of God and put them in the treasury of his gods. He was displaying them as trophies of victory. His gods defeated the God of Israel.

Defeat was crashing in on these boys from all sides. In their vulnerability, Nebuchadnezzar not only changed their names, but gave them access to his table. They had the best of his foods and wine and he invested in their education. He was moving towards them with a father's comfort and resources to cut off the connection to their lineage, culture, and God.

Hold the Line

Daniel, Hananiah, Mishael and Azariah made the request to not defile themselves by eating the meat and drinking the wine from the king's table. Several youths were taken from Israel, but only these four boys were found holding the line in the whirlwind of all that was transpiring in their life. How easy it must have been to justify eating from the king's table. What does it matter now? Our God has lost. The hope of my future is over. I must just try to survive.

Compromise of our true identity happens little by little, not in one giant leap. Culturally, eating from someone's table was a sign of communion and intimacy that affirmed the sharing of values and gods. These four boys had an identity alive on the inside of them that kept making faithful decisions, regardless of what others were doing or the luring comfort made available by the king.

I read this fable the other day about luring comfort. A lady had a huge python snake for a pet and it stopped eating and began to get very "snuggly" in the evenings. She took it to the vet and described the odd behavior, thinking it was sick. The wide-eyed vet explained that her "pet snake" stopped eating and started stretching out to "snuggle" the length of her in order to measure her for its next, large meal.

I cringed! When we live in compromise, we're deceived into believing we're engaging with a harmless pet. When we fellowship with evil, we're blurring the lines that protect our souls from the one who came to steal, kill and destroy an entire generation, one person at a time. The spirit of shame is our enemy and he wants to live close enough to whisper lies that feel intimately true.

Our battle is not against flesh and blood (Ephesians 6:12). We are not in a war against people. Our battle is with the evil spirits, the principalities that are luring us with comfort in order to measure us for destruction. These four boys refused to get in bed with a "harmless pet," one tiny decision at a time.

Your Real Name

Hannaniah means "Beloved by the Lord." Mishael means, "Who is as God?" Azariah means, "The Lord is my help."[2] Deuteronomy 6:5-9 commanded fathers to speak into the identity of their sons and daughters:

> You shall love the Lord your God with all your heart and with all your soul and with all your might. And these words that I command you today shall be on your heart. You shall teach them diligently to your children, and shall talk of them when you sit in your house, and when you walk by the way, and when you lie down, and when you rise. You shall bind them as a sign on your hand, and they shall be as frontlets between your eyes. You shall write them on the doorposts of your house and on your gates (ESV).

Every day, Hananiah heard his father speak to him as the one who was beloved by the Lord. Day after day, he was the one the Lord loved. Mishael grew hearing over and over that there is no rival to His God. His identity pointed to a God who is matchless. Azariah was born into an awareness that in all things, the Lord is his help. There was no war on the inside of them over who and Whose they were.

Nebuchadnezzar gave them a new name in honor of his many gods and there is not one record of their grumbling, being offended, or disputing it. There was no need to defend what wasn't in a war. They had become the name their fathers had given them. Nebuchadnezzar could kill their family, educate them in the ways of his gods, wine and dine them, but none of it could silence the sound of their truest voice.

True Honor

These three boys found themselves thrown before King Nebuchadnezzar because they refused to bow in worship to his 9-foot statue (Daniel 3). They had just been promoted over the affairs of Babylon by their friend Daniel and were using their skillful wisdom, knowledge and competence to serve the king. They continued to draw a bold and obvious line in their service; their communion and worship belonged to their God alone.

They didn't make picket signs and march around the massive statue, shouting insults for all to hear. They also didn't justify compromise. They didn't tiptoe around the idol worship. They had values and virtues that were lived boldly and courageously, not for man to see but before their God. Our voice will always be first for Him.

We don't serve a culture "sleeping with a pet snake" by becoming famous for what we hate **or** by walking on eggshells around their statue. There is no record of the boys verbally condemning their idol worship or defending the one true God. They simply refused to compromise within their own voice. They were not afraid of offending Nebuchadnezzar. They lived with the fear of the Lord.

Honor doesn't react to culture. Honor responds from an elevated place of identity in the living God. Living from our true identity doesn't pursue an agenda to make loud the things we disagree with. It's an equal perversion of our true identity to blur the boundaries of our faith to not upset culture. We know our voice has become the sound of honor when we can go low to serve with excellence in the deepest darkness and can stand tall without compromise as one consecrated to the Lord alone.

Nebuchadnezzar, in furious rage says, "But if you do not worship, you shall immediately be cast into a burning fiery furnace. And who is the god who will deliver you out of my hands?" This is Mishael's very name, "Who is as God?"

It wasn't first their great gifts that would magnify their God. It was their *name*. It was who they were created to be that was telling the story of their God. Their voice on the earth was the sound of who and Whose they were.

They responded to Nebuchadnezzar's mocking question with, "O Nebuchadnezzar, we have no need to answer you in this matter. If this be so, our God whom we serve is able to deliver us from the burning fiery furnace, and He will deliver us out of your hand, O king. But if not, be it known to you, O king, that we will not serve your gods or worship the golden image that you have set up" (Daniel 3:16-18 ESV).

They felt no need to defend their God. Azariah's identity was shouting the nature of His God without an argument – "The Lord is my help."

Sometimes, I feel the need to defend God when I hear of His goodness and kindness being misrepresented. I then hear Him remind me, *"I am your Defender. You are not Mine."* He needs no defense when it comes to His nature. Nothing anyone thinks of Him could ever change who He is. Circumstances, evil, and opinions do not define the nature of God.

But If Not

The furnace was heated so hot that the mighty men who bound them instantly died from the heat coming off the furnace. As the boys were falling in the fire, I wonder if they thought, *This must be the,* **'But if not.'** They so confidently said, "Our God is able, He will deliver us **but if not** we still will not bow" (Daniel 3:17-18, emphasis added).

There were so many beautiful opportunities for the Lord to swoop in and deliver. Yet here they were, falling into the furnace after watching massive, mighty men instantly combust into flames.

Their faithful endurance is such an incredible example of James 1:1. "Count it all joy, my brothers, when you meet trials of various kinds, for you know that the testing of your faith produces steadfastness. And let steadfastness have its full effect, that you may be perfect and complete, lacking in nothing" (ESV).

These boys walked the trial through to the very end. Steadfastness had its full effect. We can't get the fruit of steadfastness by walking away in the middle of our story. When we feel the, "But if not" has taken place in our lives, how much does it take to question the Lord's motive towards us? Where do we stop believing the name He called us? Where do we get cynical about His help and His rich love for us?

There are so many beautiful things we can get in a moment, but the fruit of steadfastness doesn't come at the beginning of the story or even the middle. Whatever the trial and testing of your faith, make it all the way to the fire.

There's no such thing as "big" faithfulness. Faithfulness at the core is very little. These boys didn't suddenly have great faith in a huge moment. They had been making tiny decision after tiny decision, one vegetable at a time. Faithful steadfastness creates a momentum to count it all joy while "perfect, complete and full effect" is taking place in our soul.

Tarry There

Nebuchadnezzar jumps up astonished. There are four men, without harm and unbound, walking around the furnace. Their matchless God had come to help the ones He loved. Theologians call this a "theophany" when Jesus, Himself, steps into Old Testament history.[2] Nebuchadnezzar had to go near the door and shout at them to come out. They were taking a walk, in the blazing, hot furnace.

It makes me laugh as I see so much of the nature of Jesus thinking this was a great place to walk with His friends. When I'm desperate to be rescued from the fire, He comes to take a nice walk, right there in the midst of it. Psalm 23:5 says, "He prepares a table for me in the presence of my enemies" (ESV).

Their enemy was literally watching the God above all gods come and set a table to be with His people. They had refused to give away their worship or fellowship with any other god by eating at Nebuchadnezzar's table and here comes Jesus, running at the opportunity to dine with His people in the presence of their enemy.

One of my favorite hymns says, "He walks with me. He talks with me and He tells me I am His own. And the joy we share as we tarry there, none other has ever known."[3] I can't help but wonder what they talked about as they took a walk in the furnace. I can imagine Jesus laughing and chatting and reminding them, they are His own.

When our enemy, the father of lies, ridicules our identity and attempts to bind our voice up in shame forever, our Jesus sets a table. When the enemy whispers, "You're forsaken," Jesus comes to take a walk. When we find ourselves in a war, we don't first look for rescue. We look for the table and tarry there with our conquering King.

They stepped out of the fire without one hair on their head singed, not a single burn upon their cloaks, not even the smell of fire upon them. The fire had no power over them. Their story was not about the wickedness of their king, the heat of the furnace or the evil in their city. Their story was about the beauty of their God.

Zechariah 4:6 says, "Not by might, nor by power, but by my Spirit says the Lord of hosts" (ESV). Might and power are attributes of our great God, but it wasn't by His attributes. His Presence came. The overwhelming emphasis in the story wasn't even about the incredible attributes of these three giants in our faith; it was about Who they belonged to.

Yielded Worship
The nature of their God was made manifest through their yielded lives. This was the very thing Jesus came to do with His yielded life – reveal the Father. When we walk through the blazing hot trial of rejection, affliction or offense, it is to leave no residue on our soul. The smell of disappointment isn't to linger. We're not destined to walk away burned and limping. We get to walk away unbound, fully alive, drenched in the aroma of Jesus because we walked with Him and talked with Him in the heat of the trial.

The goal is not that the world around us would be impressed with the size of our trial or the wicked intent of the earthly king, but that they would see, "These men have been with Jesus" (Acts 4:13). Our story, too, is not about the trauma in our childhood or the obstacles we overcame. Our story is about the overwhelming and unending beauty of our good God.

Nebuchadnezzar said, "Blessed be the God of Shadrach, Meshach and Abednego, who has sent his angel and delivered his servants, who trusted in him, and set aside the king's command, and yielded up their bodies rather than serve and worship any god except their own God" (Daniel 3:28 ESV).

I can't help but see their lives shouting of our coming Savior who would also set aside the ways of culture, trust in the Father so wholeheartedly and yield His own body up to death.

> The devil took Jesus up and showed him all the kingdoms of the world in a moment of time and said to Him, "To you I will give all this authority and their glory, for it has been delivered to me, and I give it to whom I will. If you, then, will worship me, it will all be yours." Jesus answered, "You shall worship the Lord your God, and Him only shall you serve."
>
> Luke 4:6-8 ESV

Guarding our worship isn't an Old Testament commandment. It's the way of Jesus. The devil was offering a shortcut to get what He came for. He could have bowed for a second and ripped the keys from the devil's grip. Jesus knew He would be brutally crucified. He chose a yielded life. He was sweating blood in agony of what was to come and yelled out in surrender, "*Not my will, but Yours be done*" (Luke 22:42).

He gave His body in complete trust to the Father. A yielded life that trusts the Father is the sound of our worship and our loudest voice erupting on the earth.

The story ends with Nebuchadnezzar promoting the boys and prophesying about their God, "How great are His signs, how mighty His wonders! His kingdom is an everlasting kingdom, and His dominion endures from generation to generation" (Daniel 4:3 ESV).

The purpose of our promotion is to advance the Kingdom we represent. In all his strategy, Nebuchadnezzar thought he could wipe out the seed of Israel forever by plucking these boys from the royal family. He killed off their family, changed their name, attempted to entangle their soul with his gods and yet, the Kingdom was progressing through to the next generation. You cannot kill this seed. You cannot destroy this lineage.

"You have been born again, not of perishable seed but of imperishable, through the living and abiding word of God" (1 Peter 1:23 ESV). We have an imperishable seed alive on our insides. Come what may, it cannot be defeated. Indestructible hope is implanted in our souls.

What He has said over you, *"You are mine. You are clean. Your God is matchless,"* is telling the story about who your God is. It's not first your gifts, talents and callings. It's who He says you are that shouts His story.

When you're promoted, the seed of this everlasting Kingdom is promoted. We don't listen when shame tells us to hide from darkness and we don't listen when shame tells us to hide from a spotlight. We arise and shine in the fullness of our voice on the earth, because the seed within us cannot keep quiet. It's telling the story of a God who called us to be His own, gave us a new name and defeated all our foes.

The Father's Table
We are the sound of the dinner bell, calling sons and daughters by their true name to dine at the table of their true Father. Jesus walked the earth calling the rejected – invited; the dirty – clean; the sick – healed. He will never call us by a name He didn't give us.

Sometimes, I imagine looking Him in the eyes before any of my story took shape. I linger there to hear what He calls me and see what He sees. His eyes are the purest reflection of truth. He is looking at His dream. He was smiling before I even came to be. I am the one He wanted. I am the best of my Father. I am the fruit of His desire. It's here, in this steady gaze that we no longer come running as a slave when shame calls us by name.

The Father is calling. Like the captive people of Zion whose feet were set free, it's the sound of our laughter and the hope in our dreams that is the dinner bell leading lost sons and daughters back to the table (Psalm 126:1-3).

What we call ourselves reveals the table we've been sitting at. Babies learn language by echoing what they consistently hear. Who we consistently hear determines what we consistently believe. I believed everything shame had to say in that dark alley when I was small and six. I called myself by the same names shame hurled towards me. I am dirty. I am wrong. I am dark. I sat in that sozo chair as a grown woman, gripped with fear that underneath all the fig leaves, my shame would be found out.

I wanted one sozo, one counseling appointment, one encounter to free my heart from the pain of those names forever. I encountered the nature of Jesus who wanted to linger in my fire. He wanted to take a walk in the dark alley. He wanted to turn the lights on, remove one tiny fig leaf at a time and sit close to my shame.

He didn't want to give me a gift of redemption. He wanted to *be* my Redemption. I wanted Him to sweep me away to a field of wildflowers and defeat all my foes. He wanted to set a table in the middle of my guilt. He wanted to pull out the fine china in the muck and mire and tell me I am His own. He wanted time, the rest of time.

When we're malnourished, eating one meal at the table doesn't fill up all the vitamins and minerals that have been depleted. When my girls were tiny, I would take them to their regular well baby check-ups and fill out a questionnaire each time. They always asked if they were found eating dirt. If a child is eating dirt, they're malnourished in some way. We wouldn't work to teach a baby to stop craving dirt, remove all the dirt from our backyard or decide maybe this baby was uniquely designed to eat dirt.

Love would sit him down at the table and give him what he is truly craving; real, whole food that he's designed to be nourished by. As his little body got the iron, vitamins and minerals it needed, the craving for dirt would disappear.

When we experience cravings that are a perversion to our design, they're pointing to what is missing. Nourishment, attention and care is missing. Working to discipline away the dirt craving will never fill up the deficit. Sitting down at the Father's table and eating will satisfy what's lacking. It's not in one meal; it's in a lifestyle of proper nutrition.

Cognitive neuroscientist, Dr. Caroline Leaf, says, "All the structures of our brains and bodies are wired for love. We are made in the image of a perfect God, a God who is love" (Gen. 1:26; 1 John 4:8).[4] If we are not latched on to our God, we will latch on to something or someone else. That something will always equate to eating dirt. Sin, addiction, toxic patterns – it's all shoveling handfuls of dirt into our soul in a desperate attempt to get our healthy and pure needs met.

Our body will need food no matter how old we are or how big we grow. In the same way, our soul will have needs no matter how spiritual we become. We lift up our head out of the dirt and behold a Father who has made provision for our every need to grow healthy and strong. We are beggars no longer. We are the voice of hope on the earth because we have unlimited access to the table, to the Presence of the Father.

Shame Was Wrong, You Belong

I heard this story years ago that deeply impacted my perspective on this living full from continually feasting at His table. A little family in Europe saved everything they had to scrape together enough money to buy ship fare to sail across the ocean and begin anew in America. They had enough left over to purchase cheese and crackers to sustain them on their voyage.

Every night, they would squeeze together in their tiny ship cabin and hear the sounds of laughing and dancing coming from the dining hall as they survived on their cheese and crackers. On the last night out at sea, the father wanted to celebrate and bless his family with a meal in the dining hall, so he found the captain of the ship to inquire about the cost. The wide-eyed captain said, "You haven't been eating in the dining hall every night? It was included in the price of your fare."

What a tragedy when we live below what Jesus has purchased for us. Shame wants us to believe we don't have enough to belong in the dining hall, at the Father's table. Shame is wrong. Jesus didn't just make provision to feast when we arrive on the other side of eternity. We have access to His table along the entire journey. It is not honoring what He purchased when we work hard to not be jealous at the sound of another's abundance. He is not getting His full reward when we push through to cultivate gratitude for our cheese and crackers. He's a Father who paid an extravagant price to give us unlimited, unconditional access to belong at His table.

One of my heroes, Heidi Baker, tells of a vision she had about the American church that has also impacted me for years. We were scurrying around underneath this beautiful table, desperate for crumbs like little rats. The Father said, *"My people are settling for crumbs when I've made room for them at the table."*

If we are living on crumbs, all we can give away is crumbs. If we're hearing and believing the voice of shame, then we'll echo and perpetuate the sound of shame in our story. If we have access to the Father's table, we have more than enough. If we know the name He calls us, we know what He calls the world around us. Our voice, the pure, uninhibited sound of who and Whose we are, will be full of joy and laughter, not as a discipline we developed, but because of the dancing and dining with our good Father.

At the table, we look in His happy eyes and smile. Shame was a liar in the dark. Up high, in the brightness of our talents, strengths and successes, we will see, shame is still a liar in the light.

Chapter 4
Shame is a Liar in the Light

I GREW UP in a tiny, mill-owned town called Scotia. Redwood trees towered over the quaint, little village, tucking it away on all sides. The streets were quiet and happy with bright, green grass that stood perfect and proud along the welcoming sidewalk. The pharmacy had penny candy that was just a short bike ride away. You could toss a burrito to the town butcher and he would heat it up with cheese and pass it back wrapped in plastic.

As you turned the corner on Main Street, there was an old, historic train parked for good next to the Redwood Museum. I pretended to drive that old train for years of my life. Every day I walked over the bridge and yelled, "hello" to my Gramps who was pulling redwood logs through the duck pond. I always felt a burst of that granddaughter type of pride walking by day after day. *I know him.*

The town whistle blew several times a day, letting us know dad was coming or going. It was like the familiar hum in an airplane that no one drew attention to, but everyone heard. The sound of steady assurance that all is well. The heroes were faithfully making our little world go round in those big, brown boots with their miles of laces.

If you raced up the steep hill, lined with the matching houses, you would see at the tip top, crowned there in glory, the town gym. It was magic. I would fling wide those double doors and breathe in the sweet smell of chlorine and feel so simply happy. It was home. For years, my favorite was to go right to the swimming pool. I would run past the ice-cold water fountain, down the hall, speed through the bathroom in hopes of avoiding awkward moments with naked ladies and jump into the heated pool. Then one day, I fell in love, and for the rest of my gym days, I would go left to the basketball court.

I didn't know you could fall in love with a game. I had been bouncing that orange ball for as long as I could remember on those shiny, redwood floors, but I really enjoyed the gummy worms at the snack shack as much as game time.

I was in seventh grade when passion took over. Passion began to rearrange my little life. Passion picked me up and left me on that court for hours at a time. It pushed me into countless pick-up games with "the guys" and didn't even let me care that they were wildly better than me. Passion left sweat, blood and pure exhaustion on the court, day after day, in complete delight. I wasn't even aware I was practicing, sacrificing, and getting better. I just woke up every day in love with this game.

I made the varsity team my freshman year of high school. I remember suddenly feeling so visible in this game I loved. The pressure began to suffocate my passion. I would feel anxiety before games instead of excited anticipation. I would calculate everything I did wrong instead of enjoying giving it my all.

I began to practice out of a desperate need to get better. Performance creates an internal culture that defines us by what we're good at. Our worth becomes intimately connected to our talent, skills and gifts. When others are better, we are less. When we fail, our value is diminished. I didn't have an identity that was bigger than the pressure of my talent. I wasn't able to remain just a girl who loved a game in the weight of people's expectations, perceived or real.

Shame wants to suffocate your voice in the dark of your past and shame wants to suffocate your voice in the light of your success. Performance is a fig leaf serving the mission of shame. It deceives us into believing our value and identity depends on success in our giftings, callings and assignments. Shame tells us we must wear our talents like a tailor-fit coat to give us access to a life of acceptance and unconditional love.

The spirit of shame is terrified that we would discover all that Jesus won in restoring the Father's dream of a garden – that place where our voice – the sound of our identity as sons and daughters – is free to walk and talk with Him in the cool of the day, naked and unashamed. The enemy trembles at the sight of a child who just loves her Father. He knows that passion will take us places performance could never go.

Significance

The story of Gideon is the story of a man who won the war on his voice and remained just a man who loved His God – naked and unashamed. In Judges 6, the Lord finds Gideon hiding out in a winepress, beating out a tiny bit of wheat. The people of God had been shamefully treated and were starving for seven years. Every harvest, the Midianites, who outnumbered the sand on the seashore, would come with their endless camels and ravish all the produce of Israel. Commentaries say it was Jesus Himself, another theophany, who showed up to Gideon to commission him as deliverer.[1] "The Lord is with you, mighty man of valor" (Judges 6:12 ESV).

Before our success in an assignment will always come affirmation of our truest identity and a promise of His Presence. Those who know their God will carry out great exploits because we know who we are to Him and who He is to us before we've done a thing. In verse 15, we see that Gideon thought of himself as the weakest and least and Jesus walked by, in the cool of the day, with an invitation to walk with Him, naked and unashamed.

Your truest voice is not found in your tribe, birth order, success or future accomplishments and prophetic words. None of those increase or decrease the value of your voice. What you do, being the "wheat guy" in Gideon's case, doesn't determine the worth of who you are. Gideon was a mighty man of valor while hiding in the wine press, beating out wheat. The unique sound and significance of your voice comes from who you are to the Father.

There was never a moment in the life of Jesus where His significance grew. Isaiah prophesied that a Child would be born and a Son would be given (Isaiah 9:11). Before He was born from Mary's womb, the Father gave Him a name – Son. The Son of God would be called Wonderful Counselor, Mighty God, Prince of Peace, Everlasting Father.

Wise men came when He was small to bow down and worship Him in all of His significance. His gifting, favor and understanding would grow. His nose, fingers and toes would get bigger. So much in the person of Jesus would develop with time. Through every stage of His development, the voice of the Son of God was erupting on planet earth.

The significance of who He was and is and will always be, never grows bigger. Before He could strap His own sandal, as He healed the sick, when He crushed death on the third day – He was never more or less the Son of the Living God.

You will never be more or less significant than you are in this very moment because your significance will never come from what you do. So many things about you will grow. Shame wants you to believe your significance is one of them. Your significance to the Father cannot grow. The war is not on the significance of your voice. The war is on seeing and believing the truth of where our significance comes from. Our voice is set wildly free when we begin to live from our secure place of significance, not performing to prove and earn it.

Stay in the Fire

Gideon was perhaps becoming aware for the first time that He was significant to the Living God. He responded to this wild encounter with Jesus by longing to bring Him an offering. He went into his house and prepared a meal for the Lord.

Authentic encounters with Jesus always take our eyes off of what we don't have in the famine and off of our own opinions about ourselves. We can't help but have an overwhelming desire to respond to Him and His opinion. We discover our voice is something worth giving when we hear the sound of His. In the middle of a severe, seven-year famine, Gideon gives. The Lord told him to put the meal on a rock, He touched the rock with a staff and fire came up from the rock and consumed the offering.

Hundreds of years and generations later, the people of God are still putting offerings on a Rock. It's no longer a meal, a bull or a goat. It's not compartments of our life that we offer – finances, relationships, church. We offer who we are, the whole of our life's voice. We are the living sacrifice (Romans 12:1). In the wind and rain, blessing and increase, we live on the eternal Rock of Jesus. We provide the sacrifice and He makes sure we live in continual fire.

John the Baptist walked the streets declaring that One was coming who was greater than him and he wasn't even worthy to untie His sandal (Mark 1:7). He would baptize with the Holy Spirit and Fire. The Holy Spirit is our gift of fire. There is no regret in a life entirely yielded to the fire of the Holy Spirit, because fire is constantly burning up and off us what does not belong. Everything that can't withstand His fire is consumed.

It's good to hear the voices of insecurity, doubt and shame scream as they are burnt down to ashes upon this Rock. Everything alive inside of you that is not the nature of Jesus is to burn in the fire of the Holy Spirit. Less of you is not the goal of the fire. The real, authentic you is the goal of the fire. The uninhibited sound of who you are, your voice, can only be discovered inside the fire of the Holy Spirit. If it were up to us to determine and discover our truest identity, we would spend our lives hiding in wine presses, believing that's where we'll always belong.

What a tragedy when we use our freedom to avoid fire. We're free to walk away from situations where we feel insecure, rejected or offended. We can create a life that constantly avoids what is supposed to be put as an offering on the Rock and consumed by the nature of Jesus. Remaining in the fire when it's hot, expensive and painful is what produces in us a life of resurrection power.

As a new creation alive in Jesus, our job is not to spend our lives working on our old man, old habits, impure motives and on and on. Our job is to yield to the Presence of the Holy Spirit. We grow by surrender to Him. Our true voice rises and relentlessly rings down into every valley and up on every mountain as old thinking is burned away, no longer suffocating the sound of our freedom in Christ. Our greatest weapon in this war is our yielded surrender to the fire of the Holy Spirit upon the Rock of the nature of Jesus.

Fire is Personal

One of my favorite seasons of learning to yield to fire was when I was eighteen, trying to decide what to do with my life. For as long as I could remember, I had a deep desire to do something significant. I remember thinking about different careers. I would picture a life given to that job or that thing and follow it all the way to the end of my days to see if it would satisfy this dream of significance.

The craving for significance grew as an eighteen year-old, with the season of transition and decisions on the horizon. I believed my gifts and talents were what made me stand out and gave me significance. Like with basketball, I seemed to do well, and felt the pressure of performance tying my worth to a deep need to continue to do well. I felt believed in by the people around me and I cared deeply about being seen as successful.

I knew without a doubt I would go to college right out of high school. I moved to L.A. from my tiny little town to study my way into something awesome. I was loving everything about college life. Mid-year, I came back early from winter break to play basketball and was the only student on my dorm floor for a few weeks. One night, I came in from practice, unaware that my life was about to radically change.

I stepped into a Presence I had never experienced before, waiting there in my room. I fell to my knees and my heart began to race. I was overwhelmed with the reality that I didn't know what I was tasting even existed. It felt like the tangible hope and atmosphere of heaven was all around me. My heart melted like a puddle inside the manifested Presence of God. He was walking by in the cool of my day.

A picture came before my eyes and I saw myself and my now husband standing in front of Bethel Church in Redding, California. I knew a little bit about Bethel, but not much. In that simple picture, I knew without any words being exchanged that I was to withdraw from college and apply to Bethel School of Supernatural Ministry. I responded with ten thousand "yeses" in the Presence of Jesus. I couldn't help but be moved by a deep desire to follow Him anywhere.

It took a couple days until fear began to grip my soul. Bethel, at the time, didn't have an "awesome and significant" reputation in most of my personal world. The glimmer of potential I thought I perceived in the world's eye as they looked at me changed to a sigh of disappointment. I was withdrawing from big, important college to apply to this tiny, ministry school in a tiny town. Tiny in my mind meant tiny in significance. I was about to learn that so much of what was tiny in my eyes was enormous in the eyes of Jesus.

Jesus had come to make an exchange in my life. He came for my big ambition. He came looking for what I thought defined my voice, life and future. His idea of significance was wildly different than mine. Chasing significance will never lead us to living a significant life.

My beliefs about what made me significant and my ambition to get there were being placed on the Rock. My achievements and potential were being handed over to Jesus who wanted my whole life. My deep care over the opinions of people and everything I thought gave me purpose was heading into a season of being burned away.

Following Jesus is intended to be intensely personal. The day He's telling me to withdraw from college, He's probably telling the friend next to me to apply for college. He sees what we uniquely need to truly live free and fully alive. He alone knows what's muzzling up our voice and keeping us stuck under a lid.

Fire is intensely personal, because our true sound can never be found by echoing the sound of the incredible person next to us. He only invites us into fires that burn up muzzles, lids, and echoes until we are refined into the purest sound of who our Father says we are in every area of our lives.

A few weeks after I decided to withdraw from college, I was tossing and turning the night before my nineteenth birthday. I heard Jesus ask me to not buy clothes for my entire nineteenth year. The wrestle was real as I lay there on my dorm bed. So much of my value rested in my appearance and it was screaming at the sight of the fire. I didn't know how much of my confidence rose and fell depending on how I felt about my physical appearance. Loving fashion is wonderful. You can't, though, truly love something that you desperately need inside. You can't enjoy good gifts if your value is hinging upon them in your life.

I slid off my bed onto my knees. My heart was racing again, but differently this time. I opened my hand in a surrendered "yes" and felt the lies of my worth screaming inside. It was a good day to let it die. I'd felt ridiculous so many moments that year. I let myself feel insecure instead of excusing how I looked and talking my way into feeling better about my appearance.

Sometimes we prolong old mindsets passing away because we talk dead things into life. It's like that dangling loose tooth. We just have to rip it off and look odd as we wait for new life to grow in the empty space.

The goal is not to love the dying on the Rock. The goal is to love clinging to the resurrected life we were born for. The Father began to speak His life and truth into these places in my heart and I could feel new life sprouting up where there were once muzzles and lids.

I remember one afternoon, studying on my dorm bed and suddenly noticing my pinky toe as if for the first time. Tiny, little, insignificant toe in my mind.

"Did you know I fashioned that toe? Did you know I gave My best when I created your pinky toe? Look at that toe!"

His delight shocked me. Of all the things He could've affirmed, He started with my pinky toe. The tiniest parts of who we are have been fashioned on purpose from His heart and are therefore, eternally significant. At some point, we have to decide who gets to define our significance, voice and value. Does culture get to decide? Do the comments from others get to choose? Does your own opinion hold the highest worth?

After I had my first baby, I was mesmerized with her tiny toes. The world would stop just so I could take in her little feet. I wanted to memorize every moment as those toes would grow. It made sense then, like never before. No matter how big we get, our Father still gets caught up in our tiny toe.

I had no idea how free He wanted me to be that night before becoming nineteen. I have fallen in love with opportunities to say "yes" in the fire. The fire brings out the best me. The fire burns away every opinion, lid and lie until the sound of His voice is the only one defining mine.

Last year, one of my students at BASSM came up to me, teary-eyed. The Father told her to give me $1,000 to go shopping. I was so blessed. I went on a shopping spree and rang in turning thirty-five. Sixteen years later, the Father had His mind on that time I wrestled to yield in the dark. When the war within is won and long gone, He is still treasuring the "yes." Goodness is always His intention. Rewarding His children is ever on His mind. I can't help but look for places to surrender and throw my whole world into His fire.

Barley Loaf

The source of Gideon's confidence had to be put in the fire. "The Lord said to Gideon, 'The people with you are too many for me to give the Midianites into their hand, lest Israel boast over me, saying, 'My own hand has saved me'" (Judges 7:2 ESV). Gideon's army of 32,000 was taken all the way down to 300 in the face of 135,000 Midianites. Gideon felt afraid. The Lord intended to burn away his fear by allowing him to hear the voice of his enemy. Gideon went into the enemy's camp and heard a man telling a dream to his comrade.

> And he said, "Behold, I dreamed a dream, and behold, a cake of barley bread tumbled into the camp of Midian and came to the tent and struck it so that it fell and turned it upside down, so that the tent lay flat." And his comrade answered, "This is no other than the sword of Gideon the son of Joash, a man of Israel; God has given into his hand Midian and all the camp." As soon as Gideon heard the telling of the dream and its interpretation, he worshiped.
>
> Judges 7:13-15 ESV

The enemy was confident they would be defeated by a barley loaf before Gideon was! A barley cake tumbled into the camp and caused the camp to be turned upside down and fall flat. It obviously wasn't the strength of Gideon's army that had been reduced to 300, or the way he tore down the altar of Baal in the night. It wasn't Gideon dressed up in tights and a superhero cape rolling through the camp. It was his most natural state. The enemy was identifying him as the one found by the Lord in the winepress. The enemy was afraid of the barley guy! When Gideon heard it, he worshiped. The Bible says the Spirit of God clothed him. He would wear God as his only confidence.

The enemy doesn't shudder at our numbers. He doesn't feel afraid of our successes, titles or talents. Our enemy, the devil, is afraid of one man who doesn't dress himself up with anything but the Spirit of God. He's afraid of one woman who knows it's not shouting louder that gives her voice power, but the Spirit of God alone blowing through the sound of her life.

Gideon's victory was dependent on his ability to remain the barley loaf found by the Lord. Our victory, too, is found in our ability to remain just a child in passionate love and complete dependence on our God. The pressure to win and sustain victory is intended to remain on Him.

When the pressure remains on the Lord, the victory will belong to the Lord and we will never say, "My own hand has saved me." The first and most significant wrestle in the war is always over our worship; a fixed gaze that magnifies and obeys our God above all else. He's the One who flips the enemy's camp upside down with a wobbly barley loaf like me and you.

Clothed in His Presence

When the people of God defeated the Midianites, they shouted, "For the Lord and for Gideon" (Judges 7:18 ESV). The Lord was worth fighting for and Gideon was worth fighting for. When everyone was blinded by the abundance of the enemy, Gideon became like a lit-up city on a hill. He was visible, had a voice, and was unashamedly living out the assignment the Lord had given him.

Gideon's success was everyone's success. Gideon's breakthrough from the silence in the winepress to the bold sound of the Spirit of God blowing freedom and victory through his life was everyone's breakthrough. Everyone benefited from the uninhibited sound of who and Whose he was. Gideon wasn't uniquely gifted and special and so God wanted to clothe him. God wanted him and so he was uniquely gifted and special. The least in the Kingdom of Heaven is actually greater than Gideon (Matthew 11:11). You are special, right now, because God wants you.

Every born-again believer is to be clothed by the Spirit of God. We don't wear our talents or success. We don't shout louder and conjure up fake power. We stand before our God, naked and unashamed, clothed by His Presence alone. There is no lid for how high we can rise when the pressure remains on the Lord. We are called to unashamedly be the city on the hill, the voice that summons the people of God to the right war.

No one would have benefitted from Gideon apologizing for being worth fighting for. When we don't use our callings and assignments to define our worth, they become the gift that frees the sound of everyone around us to increase.

Without Apology

One afternoon, in a sweaty basketball jersey, I saw again the importance of unashamedly being our best like Gideon modeled so well. During practice, first string wore white and second string wore blue. We would scrimmage, run our offense, and work hard for game day.

A girl in white was playing defense, guarding her friend in blue who had the ball. She swatted the ball away and made her friend's offense look bad. Under her breath she said, "Sorry."

My coach heard. His clipboard crashed to the ground. "Did you just say, 'Sorry?' Do you think her opponent is going to say sorry on game day? Do you think you're making her better with your apology?"

We all ran to the line and did sprints for what felt like an eternity. He was drilling into our sweaty, exhausted souls that no one will ever get better without our best. Our friends will never rise to the occasion in our apology or be prepared for game day by our concern of how we make them look. We're all on the same team. When you get better, we all get better. When you bring your best, we all receive the best.

We need you to show up at the table without apology in that thing you do well. You don't have to apologize for your strength or your weakness. We need people who are strong and excellent in areas where we are weak and growing. Their strength lifts lids, calls us higher and makes us better. If we feel insecure or jealous around the strengths and favor of others, we need them even more than we knew. Insecurity and jealousy serve us into an opportunity to untie our worth from the things that are never intended to define us and twist us up in comparison.

Esther is a hero in winning the war on her voice without apology. She stood shoulder to shoulder with her peers in the quest for a new queen. I'm sure they all wanted to be chosen to live the dream of the crown, robe and royalty. Nothing qualified Esther more than the others, but she found favor with the king. When she was chosen out of the masses, I wonder if everyone was happy at her favor. What a tragedy it would have been if she had declined the opportunity and tried to defer to her neighbor.

When we filter our decisions through a lens of concern about the opinions of those around us, we miss the point of favor. The favor that put the crown on Esther's head was the same favor that saved her people. Shying away from the favor of the Lord is shying away from the people we're called to serve and love.

Humility and hiding are not the same thing. Rejecting the crown, withdrawing from influence and silencing her voice would have been hiding in fear, not humility. Esther's humility lived aware of the favor and influence given to her voice. She used it to benefit the people of God who were on the brink of destruction by the evil agenda of Haman. She wrestled in the night with the wisdom of her uncle, counted the cost of her own life and became famous, to this day, for the courage in her voice that saved her people, "If I perish, I perish" (Esther 4:16 ESV).

The crown wasn't the final destination of her favor. It was the invitation for the uninhibited sound of who she was to be entirely spent on her God and His people. Her title didn't define her or cover her like a fig leaf, but served the assignment God had given her. You, too, have been given a crown and favor with a king, the King of Kings. You know you've learned the point of your favor when the sound of who and Whose you are is without apology and entirely laid down.

The Point of Favor

King Saul's son, Jonathan, knew the point of royal favor like Queen Esther. Jonathan was in line to receive the crown and potentially inherit his father's jealous insecurity along with it. King Saul was literally trying to murder David because of envy. Jonathan's soul was knit to David's and the Bible says he loved him as his own soul. There was none of his father's envy in him.

"Then Jonathan made a covenant with David, because he loved him as his own soul. And Jonathan stripped himself of the robe that was on him and gave it to David, and his armor, and even his sword and his bow and his belt" (1 Samuel 18:3-4 ESV).

Jonathan knew the authority in his voice, who he was and what he had to give. If we don't know the sound of who we really are, we will think the robe, sword, bow and belt are what make us royal. We will strive to protect it like Saul and end up with a title on the outside, but no royalty alive on the inside. A true king lives to benefit the kingdom. Jonathan was living with the heart of a king without needing the title. He wasn't *deferring* to David; he was *giving* to David. Jonathan is a prophetic picture of New Covenant kings and priests who seek first the Kingdom of heaven and love even their neighbor as their own soul. (Matthew 6:33, Mark 12:31).

There is no David without Jonathan. He literally kept David alive. He chose to use his favor, title and influence, to love his friend as his own soul. The only way to know if we own our titles or if they own us, is to lay them down in love.

Years after Jonathan had died, David was sitting as king in the fulfillment of what God had said over his life. He remembered Jonathan and called for anyone from the house of Saul that he might show kindness for the sake of his friend. A son of Jonathan, Mephibosheth, was brought to him. He had been lame since the age of five and now had a son of his own.

Mephibosheth fell at the feet of David. I'm sure David saw a bit of his old friend in his son – maybe his voice, eyes, or mannerisms. He was looking down at the legacy of Jonathan.

Mephibosheth was kneeling at David's feet, lame and full of shame. The Bible tells us he thought of himself as a dead dog (2 Samuel 9:8). In just one generation, the son of a confident and generous prince thought of himself as one who had nothing to give and no value to add.

David said to Mephibosheth, "Do not fear, for I will show you kindness for the sake of your father Jonathan, and I will restore to you all the land of Saul your father, and you shall eat at my table always" (2 Samuel 9:7 ESV).

Jonathan had pointed all his favor and influence to benefit David and now, years after he was gone, that favor would find his son. David didn't just tell him stories about his dad and give him a hug. He gave influence over the land of his lineage and favor to sit forever at his table, just like one of David's sons.

How many times can a "dead dog" eat with the king before he realizes he's actually the son of an incredible prince? For the sake of his friend, David made sure he would find out. David was using his favor and authority to lift lids on Mephibosheth's identity by honoring him as a son. Generations later, Jesus would go looking for the ones who believe they are nothing more than a dead dog. He would lift every lid silencing the truest sound of who and Whose we are by honoring us as sons with a permanent and personal seat at the Father's table for the rest of eternity.

The King of Kings, and highest standard of true royalty, laid down His entire life and spent the whole of His voice on His Father and His people. He was mocked before He was crucified (Matthew 27:27-30). An entire battalion of soldiers had gathered to demean and ridicule Him. Roman soldiers in Jerusalem were famous for playing cruel games on prisoners. He had already been scourged, beaten with a whip made of metal and bone to tear through flesh. It was likely that organs and bones were exposed after enduring such a horrific beating. Many prisoners died from the scourging itself. He could barely stand as they gathered around to mock Him.

They stripped Him down and put a scarlet robe on His back. They twisted together a crown of thorns and pushed it into His head. They put a reed in His right hand and knelt down saying, "Hail, King of the Jews!" They spit on Him. They took the reed from His hand and struck His head that was already pierced through from the thorns.

Jesus was silent. He didn't defend what was true. He knew every knee would bow, in heaven and on earth and under the earth, and every tongue would confess that He is Lord. He knew that the twenty-four elders would cast their crowns at His eternal throne and cry, "Worthy!" Yet, He said nothing.

The truth of His identity was being mocked with a robe and twisted crown and He was silent so His people would never again have to use their voice to defend who and Whose they are. He did it for you. He did it so nothing put on you and nothing taken off of you will ever define your worth. He took the shame of being mocked upon Himself so we, too, would never have anything to prove. We could live naked, unashamed and covered only with Him in the deep of our identity.

As He is, so are we in this world (1 John 4:17). John saw Him in heaven, clothed with a long robe and golden sash around His chest. The hairs of His head were white, like white wool, like snow. His eyes were like a flame of fire. His feet were like burnished bronze, refined in a furnace, and His voice was like the roar of many waters. In His right hand, he held seven stars. From His mouth came a sharp, two-edged sword and His face was like the sun shining in full strength. He is the first and the last, and the living One. He died and is alive forevermore with the keys of death and hell in His hand (Revelation 1:12-16).

You are the son of this King and He has pointed His favor ever your way. How many times will we sit at the table of King Jesus until we see there's no longer a dead dog inside of us? We are His. He put His pure crown on your head and His robe of righteousness on your back. As His voice is, so is yours – like the roar of many waters that the earth has been groaning to hear.

We are among those who use our favor, gifts and talents to live entirely spent on Him. We live from passion and let it lead us to the feet of Jesus in a way performance never could. Passion compels us to lay down our every crown, unreserved and without restraint. With the whole of our voice, we relentlessly kneel to say, "Worthy is this Lamb Who was slain for me!"

I will win the war to remain just a child who loves the King, without apology and with nothing to defend. You will too. My voice will be found in the sound of the Lamb. Yours will be too.

Chapter 5
The Sound of the Lamb

I WAS PREGNANT with my first baby, navigating rough seas of first trimester nausea. We lived in Redding, California and it was summer. Meaning, it was ridiculously hot. I left a pair of pot holders in the passenger seat in order to not touch the blazing, hot steering wheel and I applied sunscreen before work in hopes of avoiding a face burn through the car window on my short drive.

My husband, Justin, was away at a meeting and I was standing, barefoot and pregnant, on the blue, indoor-outdoor carpet in the kitchen with a blank stare.

I was hungry, but everything sounded repulsive – until I spotted the super-sized can of gravy stew. It felt like a glowing lighthouse out there on the unpredictable nauseous seas I was sailing. I opened the can, popped the lid off and caught one brief smell of the chunks of artificial meat hidden in thick, brown mush. I instantly threw up in the sink. It smelled like a terrible idea. I called it quits and headed to bed.

I woke up to the sound of Justin walking into the room. I was eager to gush my war hero story and rasped out, "Babe."

He said nothing. I said it again, "Babe."

Nothing. He was just standing there in the dark. A little annoyed, I sat up, and said, *"BABE!"*

He came into clearer focus as I saw a Man, not my husband, holding a lamb around His neck, pointing at me. My eyes were wide open, seeing in the spirit like never before. Heart-throbbing fear erupted through my body and I darted out of the room as fast as my pregnant body could run.

Jesus came into my room and I left! What? I still laugh with Him today about that time He walked in the room and everything changed, because I left. If only I'd fallen on my face and said, "Your servant is listening" or "Here I am, Lord."

Nonetheless, years later, I'm still left marked, not by my response, or lack thereof, but that He came with a lamb around His neck, pointing at me. The sound of who we are as a lamb at rest upon the shoulders of our Good Shepherd is found in the sound of who He is as the perfect Lamb of God. The Voice of the Lamb, the uninhibited sound of Who and Whose He was, was full of vulnerable trust, need and dependence on the Father. Our voice as His lamb is found inside of knowing and hearing His.

The Lamb of God
John the Baptist gave his voice to make straight the way for the voice of Jesus. Of all the things John could have pronounced at the first sight of Jesus, he chose, "Behold, the Lamb of God who takes away the sin of the world!" (John 1:23,29).

He took away the sin of the world as a yielded Lamb. The cross was put upon His shoulders and He carried the weight of His approaching death. "Like a sheep He was led to the slaughter and like a lamb before its shearer is silent, so He opens not His mouth" (Acts 8:32, ESV). Without any words spoken from His mouth, He was writing the Gospel forever into human history. He breathed His last breath and hung His thorn-pierced head. The Lamb was slain.

Joseph of Arimathea came to take away the lifeless body of Jesus. He was a rich man and a disciple. He, apparently, was never asked to sell everything he owned to follow Jesus because he was known for his wealth and had a tomb, an extremely expensive tomb, where no one had ever been laid (Matthew 27:57-60). He wasn't following his money; his money was following him as he followed Jesus.

Culturally, it was common for crucified criminals to be left for wild animals to devour. Not on Joseph's watch. His wealth would care for the body of Jesus. He would literally follow Him into His death. Joseph was the one who took the Savior of the world down from the tree.

Joseph stood before Jesus. His battered body was the overwhelming reality. Jesus was now hanging by threads of flesh. The feet that so many had fallen over for mercy, hung lifeless. Joseph was the one that knelt down in the pool of His shed blood to remove the nails pierced through the feet of mercy. He had to take the right hand of the Lamb of God and remove the nail pierced through His palm. Then His left. The lifeless weight of Jesus draped over Joseph.

The One who told the lame to walk and the blind to see with just a word was being carried lifeless to the tomb. He chose the way that needed a friend.

Joseph of Arimathea was the one who personally felt the weight of the demolished body of Jesus. He was the first to be covered in the literal blood of Jesus. He was covered in the blood that would wash away the sin of the whole world. He put the sacrifice of Jesus upon himself. We, too, live inside the sound of the Lamb by feeling the weight of His sacrifice upon our personal life.

When our arms are full of the crucified King, there's no room for self-righteous pride. What could we earn? What could we prove? He gave me His life. Surely He is worthy of the whole of mine.

He couldn't raise a finger or whisper a word. He was dead. It was the darkest hour of human history and Jesus was showing us the way of a lamb. He was needy and dependent. He committed Himself to the Father. He yielded to the Holy Spirit.

On the third day, the sting of death was crushed by the Father and Holy Spirit, resurrecting the Son. The Bible says we were crucified with Him, buried with Him and the same Spirit that raised Jesus from the dead is living and breathing within us (Galatians 2:20, Romans 8:11). We were as dead as Jesus, carried lifeless to the tomb. We were carried into death that we would also be carried into life.

> What man of you, having a hundred sheep, if he has lost one of them, does not leave the ninety-nine in the open country, and go after the one that is lost until he finds it? And when he has found it, he lays it on his shoulders, rejoicing. And when he comes home, he calls together his friend and his neighbors, saying to them, 'Rejoice with me, for I have found my sheep that was lost.' Just so, I tell you, there will be more joy in heaven over one sinner who repents than over ninety-nine righteous persons who need no repentance.

> Luke 15:3-7 ESV

The resurrected life is not a day of rescue on the shoulders of Jesus. The resurrected life is every day, remaining dependent on the Source of our life. Apart from Him, we can do nothing (John 15:5). The call of the gospel is the call to live carried and yielded on the shoulders of our Shepherd. We only do what He's doing and go where He's going because we live in and upon Him.

Jesus doesn't go to the sheep pen and throw 100 sheep upon His shoulder. He leaves the ninety-nine and looks for the one. In Luke 15, we see in the parables of this one lost sheep, one lost coin, and one prodigal son that He points all His attention to the one. He's pointing at *you*. You can hear the truth of the Gospel and respond to an altar call in a crowd, but, you cannot have a personal relationship with Jesus in a crowd. Your salvation becomes personal when you become the one He rejoices over and the one, like Joseph of Arimathea, who feels the overwhelming weight of what the sacrifice of the Lamb has done.

Weakness

The Lamb of God unapologetically needed, yielded and depended on the Father and the Holy Spirit. Jesus said in John 14:10, "Even my words are not my own but come from my Father" (TPT). His voice was inside the voice of the Father. We are not called to find a strong and powerful voice by digging a well of our own great strength. We are called to dig a deep well of need that clings to our God of great strength and in Him we find our voice. The weak *say*, "I am strong" when we live aware of where true strength comes from (Joel 3:10).

At times, I find myself terribly weak, unable to find my own strength. It feels like the weight of the whole world is plastered on my suffocated chest and I squint one eye open with dirt and a grimace on my face. Then I see Him standing there, towering over my exhausted, defeated life. He is smiling, bright and carefree. His kindness bends down to dirty, little me and whispers in my weary ear, *"Be of good cheer, I have overcome the world"* (John 16:33). All the pressure rolls off my soul. I can smile and say, "I am strong" when I'm living upon the one Who overcame the weight of the world.

When my daughter was ten, I learned to dig a deeper well of this need for Him. We found out she had to get an MRI as an investigative procedure. She was afraid and looking to me to offer a strength that was bigger than her fear.

She had to lie completely still in a tightly confined, incredibly noisy tube for thirty solid minutes. Many grown adults have a hard time with this procedure. We talked through a plan and then talked through the plan again and again until I lost count. She would imagine she was riding a horse and the loud clicking sounds were the hooves, talk to Jesus, maybe take a little nap, sing songs in her head until she ran out of songs. She had a great list to fill up the time.

When we got in the actual room, she began to feel so overwhelmed. Tears were streaming down her face and everything within her did not want to do this. The technician was so gracious and let me stay in the room with her. As she lay on the table, preparing to go into the tube, I reminded her of the list and the plan of all she would focus on. She looked at me, tears everywhere and said, "I don't care about that. I just want you."

We quickly changed the plan to thinking about every detail of the date we just went on, and that I would not look away for one second, and how she would feel me rubbing her leg the entire time. She went in teary, afraid and so brave. Sometimes the greatest picture of courage is a terrified face with a shaking voice, moving forward. She peeked her eye open a handful of times during the thirty minutes, just long enough for me to smile and motion for her to close it again.

As I stood there watching my brave girl, I barely blinked. When she would peek open her eyes to see mine, she was looking to rest her fear in me. She was looking for me to absorb what felt bigger than her. It takes enormous strength to be bigger than my children's fear, to be a resting place for their insecurity, to absorb their lack or confusion. Through trial and error, the secret I am finding to this great strength is, weakness.

My voice is strongest when I am weakest in the right place. I tell my soul not to be weak to agree with the lies of the enemy. Be entirely weak, oh my soul, before the one Lamb who made Himself eternally and unfailingly strong. Be weak to His goodness. Be undone by His kindness. Be defeated by His promise. Need Him.

He's Available to be Needed

We don't need Him as an orphan with the voice of a beggar. The Lamb of God needed the Father with the voice of a confident Son. Orphans and sons are born with the same needs, but an orphan learns shame in needs. The needs push him to the side of the road, gripping the sign of a beggar. A son learns joy in needs because the needs push him into the house to see the happy countenance of his available father.

The reality of being a child of God with an available Father became clearer the moment my first baby was laid on my chest, born with needs. I sat there, in utter and complete relief that labor was over, with a heart that was so content. I gave birth to a human being. I couldn't imagine a more fulfilling thing I could do with my life. She was mine. She was breathing on my chest.

She instantly began rooting, looking to nurse. I was amazed that a desire to nurse was already wired within her. I didn't have to teach her. She wanted something she had never tasted, but so confidently knew was for her. I couldn't help but desire to give her all of myself, without reservation.

For months she grew and received all her nourishment from my presence. My nearness was the source of her growth. In the same way, we were born again and laid upon the chest of the One we came from. Confident awareness that He has everything we need is wired within us. It's in our new nature to desire His nearness to meet our every need and be the source of our strength.

We are taught the lie of fear that He might withhold and are deceived into anxiety that there might not be enough. Brokenness teaches us that it's shameful to live with needs. Jesus said, "I am the bread of Heaven," and "I have water that will cause you to never thirst again" (John 6:51, 4:14). He wasn't breaking off a single piece of Himself to nourish us forever or giving us one drink that would satisfy us for eternity. He was saying, "My nearness will be your nourishment. I will never leave you." He would be our well and our manna in the morning. He would give us access, without reservation, every moment of every day for eternity.

Babies are never too busy to eat. They don't develop the discipline of eating. Eating is the happiest place of their tiny life. Jesus doesn't become our source of strength and nourishment by bottling up what someone else is drinking or making what He gave us yesterday last. We become aware of His nearness and our ongoing need for Him. We need Him today, tomorrow, for eternity and He couldn't be happier about it. We will never again cry out with the voice of a beggar because we have a happy, all sufficient Father.

All Sufficient

Your voice becomes the sound of a son prophesying to a groaning earth about an all sufficient Father when we see there will never be a deficit in the sacrifice of the Lamb. He finished lack. Worry is a lid on our awareness of the fullness of what Jesus has done. Guilt and shame over feeling worried and anxious will never set us free to live at rest on the shoulders of our Good Shepherd. Following our worry and listening to the concern of our heart will lead us to the deeper places where we've tied our soul to a poverty that's unaware of Whose we are.

For as long as I can remember, I unconsciously believed worry was an acceptable and expected experience I managed in hopes of not turning into a "worry wart." If you love people deeply, you will deeply worry about them, forever. The problem with that belief is the *Person* of Love never modeled worry. There has never been and never will be a quiver of worry in His voice. We can't accept as normal what He gave all to defeat. Our life honors His sacrifice when He remains the standard for everything we dream our voice to become.

One day, I was in a meeting and anxiety began welling up in my soul. I wrestled there in my chair, through the whole meeting. The next morning, I was talking to Jesus, pouring out my authentic concern (worry) that I felt in the meeting. I suddenly saw a picture of Him sitting in the same meeting, in my very chair. He looked relaxed and content with His legs crossed, eating a granola bar. Shocked, I said to Him, "You were eating a granola bar? Wait. What?" His Voice did not sound like mine.

I was tight and tense and He was light-hearted and free, eating a snack. He is the most carefree Person I've ever known and He *is* love. He's not careless, unaware or disconnected from our pain and concern; He's confident in His sufficiency.

Another day, I threw myself dramatically on my bed, worried about some issues my girls were working through. I thought, *OH, GOD! I can't worry like this for twenty more years.*

I gently heard the Father say, *"I am the best Father the world has ever seen and I have never, not one day, worried about you."*

My weary soul took a deep breath as I started running through scenes in my life. I saw good reason to worry about me, but my perfect Father, Perfect Love, never worried.

Jesus didn't just crush a spirit of worry that torments us and steals the peace in our voice. People all over the world have tools to meditate, breathing techniques and religious rituals that successfully reduce anxiety, but have nothing to do with the sufficiency of Jesus. He didn't give as the world gives. Jesus gave what the world could never give. He gave us access to the Father.

If we have access to a good, generous and limitless Father, we are rich in everything we need. I've often wrestled with worry over money and have let it lead me to the deeper place of poverty in my soul. People with millions of dollars can still wrestle in the night with anxiety over not having enough. More dollars can't put to rest the fear of one day not having enough to be cared for. We're at home in the care of the Father who doesn't need dollars to provide. He created everything we are, everything we see and experience without a single penny.

I care deeply about faithful stewardship, but we can't faithfully steward anything we've been given when a fear of lack is driving our choices. Of all the things we've been given in life to steward, His all-sufficient Presence is at the top of the list.

One day the Lord told me, *"To faithfully steward my Presence you will have to break up with poverty. I am God and I do not run out."* Worrying that the joy we have in His goodness, the revelation, healing and encounters might one day run out – it all points to a poverty of soul and a lid on our awareness of His nature. Beholding His abundant nature in all things is not optional to faithfully live the truest sound of who and Whose we are. We are the sheep of His pasture, known for the sound of our rest in Him, not for our poor and worried clenched fists.

The Needy Giver

Bill Johnson says, "The poverty spirit is a spirit of ingratitude." When we find ourselves aware that worry has led us to a place of poverty in our soul, the best thing to do is become wildly grateful for what we do have. Gratitude takes our eyes off of what we are without. When we open wide the fist poverty taught us to clench, we find there is always something there to give with faith and gratitude. A hero of our faith became famous for what she did with one tiny penny in her open hand.

Jesus sat down in the tabernacle. He was watching the rich, the respected Pharisees, give into the offering box. They were giving lots of money and He sat, unmoved. Then He saw an old widow come up to the box and put in two copper coins – the equivalent of one penny. It moved Jesus. He said she had given more than all the others combined because she gave out of her poverty. She had given all she had to live on and they gave out of their abundance. She was poor in dollars, but rich in soul (Luke 21:1-4).

She had so little and she gave to her God. It touched the heart of Jesus, the One who came to give us life and life more abundantly. He taught on the mountaintop, "Blessed are the poor in spirit, for theirs is the Kingdom of heaven" (Matthew 5:3 ESV). The way we received the abundant life in the Kingdom is the way we sustain the abundant life in the Kingdom. We were the needy widow – alone, with no strong provider and then we received the Lamb who was slain.

She saw the respected religious people putting in their big offerings. She could've compared herself to the rich and counted her penny as nothing. Comparison steals our opportunity to see and treasure a Jesus who is moved by the one tiny cent. Her penny dropped in the box and it shouted to her God. "I give up the last of my ability to care for myself. I trust in my Good Shepherd to sustain me. My God sees me. I have a Provider. My Maker is my Husband" (Isaiah 54:5). We don't know her story or even her name. We just know this poor widow became a hero of our faith because she opened her hand and gave.

Jesus came to be our source of abundant life. Abundance is found in the overflow. We are the people of more-than-enough, walking the earth like an overflowing cup, spilling out the Kingdom of Heaven as we wobble through our days. We give to the world from our abundance as the beloved Bride of Christ, but to Him, we give one tiny penny at a time. We live aware that our pennies can never measure our greatest wealth or source of provision. The only unbearable poverty is a life without Him. We are the cheerful givers who gave away the sorrow of sustaining ourselves. We are His.

When Jesus becomes our greatest source of wealth, we can't help but become His generous sound of abundance to the world around us. I couldn't help myself one Saturday night during corporate worship at Bethel Atlanta. I was wearing my favorite pair of oiled, brown, authentic Birkenstocks. I'd worn them every day since I purchased them in May to this night in July.

As I was caught up in worship, I saw a picture of myself bending down at the feet of one of my dear friends and putting my Birkenstocks on her feet. I whispered in her ear, "You will never walk alone." My heart exploded with gratitude and joy. I had a little something to give.

I walked home that night with bare feet and a full heart. For two days, I headed out the door and felt happy to miss my Birkenstocks.

Later, I found out during that exact service, someone handed my husband two-hundred dollars and said, "Go shopping." In the moment, he felt compelled to give the money away.

On Tuesday, he would take me shopping and give it away, to his bride. With that ridiculous happiness that looks through his blue eyes into my soul, he bought me oiled-brown, authentic Birkenstocks.

They used to be a pair of shoes that I loved. Now, I slip them onto my feet and I hear the sound of my ridiculously happy Bridegroom, Jesus, *"You, my love, will never walk alone."*

We open wide our hand with gratitude and give without reservation because He gives without reservation. We love without reservation because His love for us will never run out. Our voice no longer quivers with concern when we are at rest in His Voice of endless abundance.

He Keeps Talking

We don't hear His voice and learn to rest in it because of something special about our ears. We hear Him because He's speaking and He put us close enough to hear, as close as His shoulder. We are near enough for every whisper, in every season.

"The sheep hear His voice, and He calls His own sheep by name and leads them out. When He has brought out all his own, He goes before them, and the sheep follow Him, for they know His voice" (John 10:3-4 ESV).

I've never heard better by trying to hear better. Jesus said, "He who has ears to hear, let him hear" (Matthew 11:14). We haven't been born again without ears. We all have ears to hear.

When babies are developing in the womb, they are not working hard to grow ears. The mother is providing everything necessary to grow. We have been put *in* Christ as a new creation. We have ears to hear because, in His goodness, He has provided everything necessary for us to grow healthy and whole. We don't strive to develop; we remain in Him.

Our ability to hear is found in the nature of our Father. We hear because of who He is, not because of a gift or skill we developed. We, like children, are growing in our understanding of His language. His kindness can be a foreign sound. His goodness and mercy is a new language we must learn. Our capacity to understand and our ability to talk just like Him grow. But we don't take a night class and study a book. We learn just like babies. We learn because our Father keeps speaking. He keeps looking into our tiny eyes and making foreign sounds with a ridiculous smile on His face, whether we understand or not. Our voice is, eventually, found inside the sound of His.

One of a Kind Love
As we grow, we find He has waited with expectation to hear the sound of our voice that moves Him more than we could have ever thought or known. I learned this in one of the most profound dreams of my life thus far, when my second daughter, Ava, was tiny. In the dream, our little family of four got out of an airplane, stepping into the most mystical place. We were floating through this thick atmosphere, doing flips and spins in the air.

Justin and I walked into this simple room with two chairs and a little table. A fish bowl was sitting on the table with a single, grey fish swimming around. We sat, delighting and gushing over our little fish. It was Ava. To the normal eye, she was a plain, grey fish. To us, she was everything. She was ours.

A dragonfly type of creature fluttered into the room and began gently landing on our shoulders then on our noses. Justin and I looked at each other at the exact same time and said, "Is this the love of God?"

Just then, the dragonfly creature went over to the fish and stung it. She instantly died and our hearts broke with grief over our girl.

Suddenly, a portal opened up over the small fish bowl and hundreds of fish that looked just like her began spilling out. The bowl was overflowing. We felt happy about the fish and heart-wrenching grief at the same time over our Ava.

We went into the next room and there were several portals opening up, pouring out thousands of fish that could fly. We were in awe, but our hearts were heavy with sorrow.

The last feeling in the dream was the weight of her absence. No matter how many fish looked just like her, mystical or profound, not one could replace or fulfill the longing in my heart for my Ava. Then I woke up.

The love of God gave His "only begotten Son" so we could be born again into the **same** love the Father has for the Son (John 3:16, 15:9). That phrase *only begotten* speaks of being one of a kind and unique. We are not unique in His love because we are a bright purple fish and the rest of the world is boring grey. We are not one of a kind because we have a supernatural gift to fly out of portals. We are unique and one of a kind because He is our Father and to a father, every son and daughter is profoundly unique.

Earthly parents were created with the natural capacity to love their children as irreplaceable little people walking around planet earth. How much infinitely more does our perfect heavenly Father possess that capacity who made us in His image?

In a crowd of ten thousand, my daughter will stand out for the rest of time because she's mine. Endless fish can surround her, but none could ever replace her. Every year, when I go watch the school play, I'm not looking for the one student who's the most talented. I'm looking for the one who belongs to me. Performance, my girl doing her best, is important to me, but it's never what makes my child stand out as unique. In a world full of beautiful, brilliant people, you are *one of a kind* because you are His.

I remember sitting one afternoon in the back of my second year, school of ministry class, having no idea what made me unique. Our leader invited anyone up who wanted to come pray on the microphone during a spontaneous time. I listened to powerful people pray the most beautiful prayers and thought, *There's nothing left for me to say. They can say it far better and more profound than me.* I sat silent that day.

I was unaware that I was thinking like an orphan. Orphans think, "I have to be the best to stand out. I need to be awesome to be worthy to speak. I have to be the loudest to be heard."

When we realize we come from a Father, we realize why our voice is so uniquely valuable. For generations, people have been shouting, singing, and declaring their love for God, but no one in all of history could ever step into your story as His child and say it *as* you or *for* you. Your voice moves Him because it's your voice, and billions of voices could never replace that. He's pointing at you, the lamb at rest upon His shoulder, to speak.

When you see He has eternally pointed His affection and desire for connection your way, you discover the point of your voice.

Chapter 6
The Point of Your Voice

I TIPTOED INTO bed, slid under the covers and barely took a breath so as not to move my body an inch. A tiny, cranky, baby was asleep next to me, finally. She had a cold. Her toddler-sister had a cold before that. I had a cold before that and Justin had a cold before that. We were all exhausted. My greatest life goal was not to wake the baby. I was too tired to have an ounce of ambition beyond sleeping longer than five minutes.

I suddenly heard a tapping on the window that the baby was sleeping right in front of. Rage erupted in my soul like a crazy wildfire. He tapped again.

My husband forgot his keys and was attempting to get me out of bed to unlock the door for him. I was screaming demeaning insults in my head, to not wake the baby.

I just get our stuffy nosed, exhausted, cranky baby asleep and you're tapping at the window she's right in front of? Are you kidding me? I am keeping us all alive and you can't even be responsible enough to remember your keys? Ridiculous.

He went from the window to the front of the house. I saw him knocking at the door with the keys in his hand. Then I woke up. I was so confused. The baby was still asleep in the dark quiet.

I got out of bed and saw my husband brushing his teeth. "Hi, Babe."

It was a dream! I lay back down and heard a tender, familiar voice. *"You've locked him out and you're blaming him for not coming in."*

The Father was correcting me. I love it when He does that. I always feel so cared for. I was my problem. Not my husband, my two needy children, their colds, or our lack of sleep. It was me. My husband was trying to get in – to see and know me – and my anger was locking him out. When we are shutting out the people closest to us from the truest sound of our voice, we are most definitely, consciously or unconsciously, shutting the Lord out as well. The point of our voice is first for intimacy and the war is to keep us from moving towards the intimate connection we were born for.

Solomon 2:14 says, "O my dove, in the clefts of the rock, in the crannies of the cliff, let me see your face, let me hear your voice, for your voice is sweet, and your face is lovely" (ESV).

Jesus wants to see your face and hear your voice. He stands at the door and knocks so He can come in and dine with us (Revelation 3:20). Danny Silk, author of *Keep Your Love On,* says, "Intimacy is into me you see, **because I showed you.**" No one can unlock the door, reveal your true voice, and be visible for you.

If it feels like our intimacy with God is a locked door, He is not the problem. I didn't know my anger was isolating me and silencing the sound of intimate connection in my life. Anger felt like my truest voice, my most natural, automatic response. I no longer saw an option to choose something besides anger. When I felt afraid, sad, or powerless, anger was my trusted friend to keep me safe. For as long as I could remember, I felt big and in control when I was angry.

Sometimes, we pick up habits – ways of coping that grow with us until they feel woven as one with who we are. Anger was insulating a little girl tucked away deep in my soul who wrestled to feel safe. As I grew, that anger became a thief, isolating me from real intimacy. It tethered me to self-pity as a false comfort in the loneliness and fear. Self-pity intends to keep us stuck and silent by perpetuating the lie that we are powerless to change the quality of our inner life. My husband says, "You can tell you are dealing with a spirit when it feels like you have no choices." In the anger and pity, I believed I had no choices.

Our inner life is either moving us towards powerful connection with Jesus or away from Him. Our truest voice is set free from the inside out. We are transformed from the toxic patterns that feel forever a part of us by renewing our mind, learning to think like Jesus thinks (Romans 12:2). Jesus chose anger at times, but never to create fake safety and fake power around His soul. He had reasons beyond measure to blame others and feel sorry for Himself, yet everything He did, He chose to do, fully responsible for His own life. The spirit of slavery wants you to believe you cannot change; you are silent and have no choices. The Gospel set your voice free to always have the choice to cry, "Abba, Father" and move towards Him (Romans 8:15).

Twelve-Year Journey

There's a story in the Bible that gives us a glimpse into a woman's powerful, inner life that moved her voice towards Jesus. She had been bleeding for twelve years. She spent all her living on physicians, trying to get well, and nothing worked. Levitical law tells us that culturally, she was considered unclean and impure for every single day of those twelve years. The bed she laid on, the seat she sat on, anything she touched was considered contaminated. If anyone touched not just her, but even the items she touched, they were considered unclean and unable to worship for a period of time (Matthew 9, Mark 5, Luke 8).

We can imagine how much this illness stole from her relationships, resources and dreams. Her daily life had been radically affected by this perpetual bleeding for twelve years – 4,380 days. The Bible says she heard reports about Jesus. She heard about the miracle worker who did astonishing things. Nothing was impossible with Him.

We don't even know this woman's name, but we get a glimpse of her thought life. "If I could just touch the hem of His garment, I will be healed" (Matthew 9:21).

She believed what she heard. She hadn't grown cynical and hard. Twelve years of an intense struggle and she still had room for hope and faith. She wasn't supposed to be out in society. She could hide in the crowd. Be invisible. Press in and push through all the people. She would touch just His garment and leave free – finally free.

Day four thousand, three hundred, eighty-ONE had come. She was mixed in with the masses. The Bible says it was a great crowd that thronged and pushed about Him on all sides (Mark 5:24). Suddenly, a ruler of the synagogue, someone with a title and known name, Jairus, falls desperate at the feet of Jesus.

His twelve year-old daughter was sick to the point of death. He, too, had been in a twelve-year process. We see a father's relentless love in the way he laid aside his title, position and the religious opinions of his peers to fall humbly at the feet of Jesus on behalf of his daughter. Jesus, matchless in mercy, gets up and follows this desperate father.

The massive crowd was seeing Jesus give His "yes" to Jairus. He was walking away. The last Hope of the woman with the issue of blood was walking away. There are so many things she could have chosen to do with her thought life in this moment.

Her story had no father blazing a trail to Jesus and throwing himself at His feet on her behalf. She was alone, an outcast, without a title or important name. She could have hung her head and turned around.

Self-pity wants to steal the five steps between you and Jesus. It shouts to draw our attention to what we do not have. It whispers, "Meditate on every injustice and lose yourself in what went wrong. Stay safe by holding disappointment close." It strips us of our power and steals our hope for a future.

Everyone in the massive crowd wanted something from Jesus. She stands out with this one thought, "If I could just touch the hem of His garment." There are so many things we can't control – Jesus, the crowd, the illness in our body. The one thing we will always control is the thoughts we choose to think.

We, alone, choose what to meditate on and behold in our mind. I love reading Dr. Caroline Leaf's research on how the thoughts we think profoundly affect every cell of our body.[1] Imagine the cells rushing towards Hope with this woman's one thought!

She touches the fringe of His garment and instantly the flow of blood is dried up and she is healed of her disease. Jesus feels that power has gone out from Him and yells out, "Who touched me?"

The disciples, squished amongst the crowd, basically respond with, "Everyone is touching you!" (Mark 5:30-31). Jesus begins looking for the one who touched Him.

The woman, knowing what had happened to her, came in fear and trembling and fell down before Him. She told Him the whole truth. She just touched countless people in that crowd as an unclean woman. She just touched the purest Person to ever walk the earth as an unclean woman. She had broken the law to get to Jesus. She thought she could sneak in, take her miracle from Him and sneak out.

Jesus took time to hear the whole truth, her whole story. Jairus, his little girl, the disciples and the crowd all wait. Jesus responds by addressing her as "Daughter." He came to reveal the Father. He came to reveal *her* Father. There isn't a greater title on earth than to be called a child of God.

She wasn't invisible. The Son of God, Himself, blazed a trail of access for her to the Father. Daughters receive. She touched His garment and He absorbed her disease. Bill Johnson of Bethel Church says, "In the Old Testament, if you touch what is unclean, you become unclean. In the New Testament, if you touch what is unclean, it becomes clean."

Jesus was showing the world, "You can touch Me. Touch Me in your shame, your pain and your sin. Touch Me and I will make you clean." He refused to let her sneak away thinking she took something from Him. She didn't take from Jesus. He gave.

As Jesus is affirming her faith and blessing her life to be full of peace, He overhears someone coming from Jairus' house to announce his daughter is dead. They say, "Why trouble the Teacher any further?" (Mark 5:35 ESV).

Jesus interrupts the conversation, looks at Jairus and says, "Do not fear, only believe." I imagine Jairus was eternally thankful that Jesus interrupted the conversation. Jairus also had opportunity to walk away believing he was *trouble* to Jesus, but the exact opposite was true. Jesus wanted and chose to walk with him all the way to his house and raise his little girl back to life.

Jairus didn't get less because he was a Pharisee with a title. Jesus gave him access to who He was in the same measure He gave the woman. Jesus walked the earth unmoved by titles, agendas, crowds or names. His internal world was moved by compassion. He only did what He saw His Father doing. We are not trouble to Jesus and we are not taking something from Him that He doesn't want to give.

You Are Always With Me

No matter where we are in our inner life process, we are not trouble to Jesus. He stands at the door and knocks, desiring to come in to dine. The first point of your voice is for intimacy because it's what He's knocking on the door for. Your process will never change His desire.

Jesus told a parable about a father and his two sons to reveal His unchanging nature that desires intimate connection (Luke 15:11-32). The youngest son asked for his inheritance and left his father's house, making terrible choices. He didn't just wake up one day and decide for the first time to disconnect from his father in such an extreme and painful way. His inner life of thoughts and emotional responses were pushing him away from intimacy, one thought at a time.

The elder brother was offended by the generosity of his father when he welcomed home his wayward brother. His inner life pushed him out to the field, refusing to come in and celebrate. Both of the boys developed a thought life somewhere along the way that missed treasuring the best thing about living in the father's house.

The father said to the offended elder brother out in the field, "Son, you are always with me, and all that is mine is yours" (Luke 15:31 ESV).

Ten thousand parties could never touch the most extravagant generosity of *always* having access to connection in His Presence. All the dollars in a rich inheritance are like eating out of a pig's trough compared to the wealth of living in intimacy with the Father. The best thing about living in the Father's house, is the Father. He finds us on the road and out in the field, withholding none of Himself, none of the time.

It's our own internal reality that moves us toward intimacy with Him or away from it.

Our great responsibility in "watching over our heart with all diligence" is protecting our value for His Presence so we find ourselves living in the greatest destiny of our voice, to know and be known by Him (Proverbs 3).

Entering the Kingdom means becoming like a child and one of the most beautiful attributes of childlikeness is a relentless value for presence. When a child is born into healthy attachment, her parents are the absolute prize of her little life. I have barely gone to the bathroom by myself in the last twelve years because everywhere I turn, there they are, wanting to be near. We, too, follow our Father around the house because our happiest place is wherever He is.

I saw the joyful, childlike value for presence early one morning when we woke our girls up with a fun surprise. We were going to Disney World, that day. They screamed and cheered and celebrated their way to the car. About two hours into the drive, our three year-old asked, "Where are we going again? Home Depot?"

We all had a good laugh. She was over the moon with joy to the point of dancing and she thought we were going to Home Depot! Her joy wasn't coming from the extravagant thing we were doing, but in who she was going with. The Presence of the Father is the main event; the ring, robe, and party will always be just the cherry on top. The point of your voice is first to cry, "Abba, Father" because to a child, everything else pales when His presence is in the room.

Equal Access

The other day, our family of six piled on a golf cart to ride through the gorgeous Peachtree City paths to one of our favorite stores. We were walking around, enjoying some family time. Justin decided to buy one of the girls some Shopkins, her current obsession. It was a bit out of character to buy something for just one of the four of them, spontaneously like that. We got back in the golf cart and she was filled with glee and our littlest was filled with tears. She wanted a toy, too. Justin scooped her up onto his lap and let her "drive" the golf cart as he talked her through it. I watched as his presence was her comfort.

Our soul becomes troubled when we need toys, gifts and things to prove that the love of the Father is present in our life. Family around this Father is not everyone receiving the same gifts, talents, and blessings. Family around this

Father is everyone receiving the same *access* to His Presence. Your voice has equal access at His table.

The deepest desire of the fatherless is not for more toys, a bigger party, or a nicer robe. The fatherless desire a *father*. Our voice celebrating the sound of a party, gifts and toys of our brother is found in our awareness that we are always with Him. If your inner life feels stuck on what others got and you did not, move towards Him. On His lap, you don't get scolded for your tears and fears. They're absorbed by who He is for you, and that will always be bigger than what He gives to you.

The Mind of Christ

The disciples modeled a value for Presence and learned the point of their voice through their access to Jesus. Jesus walked by before they were disciples and said, "Follow Me!" They left their nets, their fish, their fathers, their entire lives and followed Him. Jesus didn't lay out a plan. He didn't present points of why they should come. He didn't even introduce Himself. Something inside of those men wanted to be with Jesus. They did that one thing we teach our children not to do – follow a stranger! When He was hard to understand and the crowds were leaving in masses, Jesus asked His twelve, "Do you want to go, too?" (John 6:67-68).

Peter responded, "Where would we go?"

The Presence of Jesus had become their life. Every day they woke up with one ambition – be where Jesus was. They didn't learn the ways of Jesus because they studied Him in a book. They lived with Him. They knew what His morning voice sounded like. They could grab His sandals out of a pile and toss them His way. They knew what made Him laugh and what made Him cry.

They didn't receive the mind of Christ as a spiritual gift. They saw and heard the way He thought. They were constantly having to adjust their inner world to live with Him. When they thought the Savior of the whole world would be too busy for children, they bumped into His thought life. They heard the tone of His voice while He blessed tiny people. When they genuinely thought it would be a good idea to call down fire on a city, they saw the look on His face before they heard His rebuke. Their inner life was transformed by the renewing of their minds, but it didn't come from spiritual discipline. It came from living in the Presence of Jesus. They didn't wait until their voice sounded like His to live with Him. Their voice began to sound like His *by* living with Him.

Jesus is *Immanuel, God with us*. He walked the earth being with His people. We often see Him in the New Testament, reclining at the table of Pharisees, tax collectors, sinners and friends. That word reclining literally means, *"to lay."* Culturally, there weren't chairs around tables, but bed-like couches.[2] When we see John, the disciple Jesus loved, laying His head on the chest of Jesus, he wasn't awkwardly leaning over from a chair. He was lying beside Him at the table (John 13:23).

Jesus came that His Presence with us would be our healing in every part of our inner process. I love how Bill Johnson points out that Jesus reclined at Zacchaeus' table and something inside the deceitful tax collector was compelled to give back double the money he had been stealing. Jesus didn't even verbally address his toxic and sinful pattern. The Presence of Jesus made Him whole – *God with him*. The sound of his voice on the earth was transformed by being near the voice of Jesus.

Enough

What a day it was when Jesus told His friends that He was going away (John 13:31-38). They had been following Him around, living in His Presence for years. They were confused. All they had known was access to Jesus.

Peter says, "Lord, why can I not follow you now? I will lay down my life for you."

Peter genuinely felt He would give His life for Jesus. He had left everything to follow Him. What a heart-wrenching moment to hear Jesus say, "Will you lay down your life for Me? Truly, truly I say to you, the rooster will not crow till you have denied Me three times" (John 13:38).

Jesus doesn't even give Peter a moment to respond to such shocking feedback before He tells Him to not be troubled. Peter is hearing that the One he has given his life to follow is leaving and every bit of confidence he has in his ability to stay connected and faithful to Jesus will fail; but, Peter, "Don't be troubled." If there was ever a time for Peter to be troubled, this was it.

Jesus said in that moment, "Let not your heart be troubled. Believe in God, believe also in Me. In my Father's house are many rooms. If it were not so, would I have told you that I go to prepare a place for you? And if I go and prepare a place for you, I will come again and will take you to myself, that where I am you may be also. And you know the way to where I am going" (John 14:1-4 ESV).

I can just imagine the men looking around at each other, confused. Thomas spoke up, "Lord, we do not know where you are going. How can we know the way?"

Jesus responded, "I am the Way, and the Truth, and the Life. No one comes to the Father except through Me" (John 14:5-6 ESV).

Jesus was affirming that He was taking all the pressure upon Himself. Peter will fail; Jesus was aware and would absorb all his insufficiency. Jesus came to manifest the heart of His Father. God wanted to *be* with His people. He didn't just want to be a visitor. He wanted to live intimately with His people; walk, talk and recline together in the cool of the day.

We needed someone bigger than our sin, failure, and unhealthy patterns to give us access to eternal connection. Jesus is the Way, the *only* Way. Our effort, like Peter's, wasn't even enough to keep us connected until morning when the rooster would crow.

In Luke 22:61, Peter had just denied Jesus for the third time and, "At that moment, the Lord, who was being led through the courtyard by his captors, turned around and gazed at Peter" (TPT).

Jesus made eye contact with Peter in the very moment his voice utterly betrayed Him, yet Jesus kept moving forward to be crucified, for him.

Peter burst into tears, ran off from the crowd, and wept bitterly. Peter wasn't enough to stay connected. The wrestle to believe we are enough distracts us from the wonder of the One who became enough for us.

One day, I was groaning before the Lord, "I feel like I wasn't enough for them."

He said, "You probably weren't."

I was shocked.

He said, "If you look to people for your affirmation, sometimes you'll be enough and sometimes you won't. If you look to Me, you will always be enough."

All of our access, everything that makes us enough, is resting in His sufficiency. We miss the beauty of who Jesus is for us when we strive to work our way into connection and Christ-likeness.

In the last chapter of the gospel of John, Peter is fishing with his friends out on the boat and resurrected Jesus shows up on the shore. There are so many things Peter could have done or felt in that moment. Of all those things, he was the only disciple that dove into the water to get to Jesus while the others brought the boat to shore. What did he know about the nature of Jesus that his first response after deep failure was to run to Him?

In the garden, our first response to sin and brokenness was to run away from the Presence. In Jesus, our first response is to run into His Presence. The broken places in our inner world become like Jesus by being with Jesus. Our true voice is found inside the sound of His.

Bondservants

Being a follower of Jesus means we go where He is and keep moving towards Him in every process of our soul. We bind ourselves to Him. Our fathers of the faith, who wrote much of the New Testament, were worthy and right to give themselves so many titles that Jesus Himself gave them, yet they chose in their letters to first call themselves *bondservants*. Paul, *bondservant* of the Lord Jesus Christ; Peter, *bondservant* of the Lord Jesus Christ; Jude, Timothy, James, *bondservant* of the Lord Jesus Christ. They bound themselves to Jesus.

We discover what it means to be a bondservant of Jesus by looking back to the Hebrew law dealing with slaves in Exodus 21.

> Now these are the rules that you shall set before them. When you buy a Hebrew slave, he shall serve six years, and in the seventh he shall go out free, for nothing. If he comes in single, he shall go out single; if he comes in married, then his wife shall go out with him. If his master gives him a wife and she bears him sons or daughters, the wife and her children shall be his master's and he shall go out alone. But if the slave plainly says, 'I love my master, my wife, and my children; I will not go out free,' then his master shall bring him to God, and he shall bring him to the door or the doorpost. And his master shall bore his ear through with an awl, and he shall be his slave forever.
>
> Exodus 21:1-7 ESV

Hebrews became slaves for a few different reasons but primarily, debt.[3] They had a debt they couldn't pay and so they were sold as a slave to pay it off. After seven years, they could go completely free of the debt unless they fell in love with their master. Bondservants used their freedom to bind themselves to their master, forever. Debt, poor choices, or terrible circumstances no longer tied them to their master. *Love* bound them.

The entire decision for a slave to become a bond-slave was based on the *goodness of the master.* They made a decision based on their experience with him in the previous seven years. They were trusting that in ten or twenty years time, through all of life's shifting seasons, their master's nature towards them would remain good, kind and generous.

James 1:7 says, "Every good gift and every perfect gift is from above, coming down from the Father of lights with whom there is no variation or shadow due to change" (ESV).

It's speaking of the unchanging nature of our Master, our Father. James is comparing the nature of the Father to the sun He created. If you carved out the sun, one million earths would fit in it. The sun is massive compared to the earth. When we experience darkness, intense weather, variation and change on the earth, it's not because the sun has stopped being a blazing hot, bright light. Something has shifted and changed in the earth's orbit, not the sun's.

The nature of our Father does not change. Good and perfect gifts have and always will originate from Him. When we become more aware of His goodness shining into the darkness of our night, it's not because He got better. He doesn't become more loving. His kindness does not grow. *We* changed. Our rain cloud, shadow, and inner world yielded to His brightness.

The call of the gospel is the call to trust in the nature of our Father. We are the bondservants who have *tasted and seen that He is good.* We are compelled not by debt or duty, but by a fierce love to give our life, the whole of our voice forever. We love our Master because He first loved us. (1 John 4:19.)

One of my favorite parables that Jesus tells about a bondservant is in Luke 17:7-10:

> Will any one of you who has a servant plowing or keeping sheep say to him when he has come in from the field, "Come at once and recline at table?" Will he not rather say to him, "Prepare supper for me, and dress properly, and serve me while I eat and drink, and afterward you will eat and drink?" Does he thank the servant because he did what was commanded? So you also, when you have done all that you were commanded, say, "We are unworthy servants; we have only done what was our duty" (ESV).

You are no longer a servant working out in the field from the duty of the debt you owe. You don't come in from the field and punch a time card, diligently working your way out of the pile of debt that will take years of labor to repay. You were bought with a price and set entirely free from the weight of your choices, sin and shame. You used your freedom to choose Him.

Your greatest destiny is no longer what you do in the field, but Who you give yourself to in the house. The first point of your free voice is for Him. We plow the field and keep the sheep because we love the Master. When we get tired and weary from the assignment we've been given, it's time to come inside and move towards Him. Not to first be served, but to first find the Master. As we serve Him, we are refreshed and nourished by His Presence. We are reminded of His kindness that won all of our affection and compelled us to give Him our lives forever.

We don't just live with a pierced ear on days when our inner world feels good. We didn't bind ourselves to our feelings. We bound ourselves to our God. When we feel in debt to this world, we look in the mirror and see our pierced ear. We gave away our life and our right to work for another. "You were bought with a price, do not become bondservants of men" (1 Corinthians 7:32 ESV).

When you have tasted the beauty of your Master, you can't help but crave the world seeing your pierced ear. "I chose to belong to Him." I gave my life, my voice, my forever, because of love. From the top of my head to the tip of my toes, I want the world to see my life is pierced. Christianity is not a chain from our voice down to our toes with ten thousand reasons for a life of constraint. Christianity is all our chains lifted high above our life, with ten thousand reasons to live a life of absolute abandon.

Jesus said He no longer calls us slaves, but friends. Friends lay down their lives for those they love (John 15:13,15). It's hard to see any difference between a bondservant and a friend because they are both laying down their life in love. True love becomes a bondservant, a true bondservant becomes a friend and a true friend becomes a bondservant.

Starting Point

The first point of our voice is for intimacy with our God, because it's only from Him that we find our voice to those around us. Our freedom in Him is our starting point in moving towards the people we are called to relentlessly serve, love and need. It's never meant to be just Jesus and me. He designed us to live from Heaven towards earth to benefit our intimacy with others. The heavenly Master we belong to is rich in every way and we move towards intimacy with people as His bondservants, bound to His wealth.

We will need to unlock the door and let people in to hear our voice, know and be known for the whole of our lives. The risks of intimacy with people become joy when our inner world finds rest in His wealth. Our souls need intimacy to thrive like our bodies need food. In the natural, the rich have a need for food and go get what their body needs with a smile on their face. They hardly even call it a need because it's such a joy to eat good food, every day.

The poor have the same need for food, but feel anxious and stuck in the powerlessness. They live surviving one meal at a time, not knowing if there will be enough to eat again tomorrow. They hold tightly to the little they have. The joy and delight is swallowed up by the fear and lack.

In the same way, we have been made rich in Love by the life we have inside of Christ, our Master. We go get what we need in intimate relationships with a smile on our face because we are wealthy beyond measure. We move towards people out in the field with joy because we live from the Master's house and have more than enough in Him.

If you feel poor, He is knocking. If your inner world feels stuck, win the war on your voice by moving towards Him. Open the door within. The first point of your voice is for intimacy. Let Him in.

"Behold, I'm standing at the door, knocking. If your heart is open to hear My voice and you open the door within, I will come in to you and feast with you, and you will feast with Me" (Revelation 3:20 TPT).

On the other side of the open door is the sound that completes your joy, the Voice of the Bridegroom.

Chapter 7
The Voice of the Bridegroom

I WAS AROUND fifteen, sitting on my bed. I had a vision flash through my mind for what felt like the first time. It was me as a bride. There were no twinkle lights or rows of roses. I was a picture of hopeless despair. My gown was dirty, battered and torn. Black makeup ran from my eyes to my chin. My hair was everywhere. The picture was worth a thousand words, all of which articulated my feeling used, unwanted and unclean.

I was marked in a moment by the vision. I didn't know I was in a war on my voice as the beloved bride of Christ. The sound of our purity is His prize. "All that He does in us is designed to make us a mature church for his pleasure, until we become a source of praise to Him - glorious and radiant, beautiful and holy, without fault or flaw" (Ephesians 5:27 TPT). Your glorious, holy and beautiful voice as His bride is found inside the voice of your Bridegroom. The dirty places that scream through our story become clean inside His perfect Light.

The Sound of the Bridegroom
In the womb, John the Baptist leapt for joy when Mary walked in the room with Jesus in her womb (Luke 1:41). John's starting point was joy over Jesus. His joy wasn't complete, though, until the day he heard the sound of his friend's voice beside His bride.

John said, "I am not the Christ, but I have been sent before Him. The one who has the bride is the Bridegroom. The friend of the bridegroom, who stands and hears him, rejoices greatly at the Bridegroom's Voice. Therefore, this joy of mine is now complete. He must increase, but I must decrease" (John 3:28-30 ESV).

If John's joy was complete just hearing the sound of the Bridegroom's voice, what did the Bridegroom's voice sound like? There was enough joy bellowing out from the voice of Jesus beside His bride that it left nothing wanting in John's joy. Jesus wasn't the sound of a distant God setting strangers free, a general drafting warriors for an army, or an incredible leader gathering as many followers as He could. He was the sound of a ridiculously happy Bridegroom coming for His bride.

Jesus was wide-eyed Love, walking the streets. His people, for the rest of time, would be known as His; the beloved Bride of Christ. He would lay down His life to win her, hold out His arm to lead her, and walk in triumph beside her with that wild look of overcoming love, blazing through His fiery, bright eyes. It's in those eyes that we see the purest reflection of who and Whose we are and break through lids in our story that want to tell us otherwise.

The Pearl
Jesus told two parables to reveal what He sees when He looks at His bride.

> A person discovered that there was hidden treasure in a field. Upon finding it, he hid it again. Because of uncovering such treasure, he was overjoyed and sold all that he possessed to buy the entire field just so he could have the treasure. Heaven's kingdom realm is also like a jewel merchant in search of rare pearls. When he discovered one very precious and exquisite pearl, he immediately gave up all he had in exchange for it.
>
> Matthew 13: 44-46 TPT

Philippians 2 tells us Jesus gave up everything, emptied Himself completely, to put on human flesh. He is the person who was overjoyed to sell everything and buy the field to have the treasure and He is the merchant who discovered the pearl and gave up all to have it. We can't treasure Jesus as the most precious and exquisite pearl of our life until we first become the pearl He found under all the dirt and bought with the whole of His life. "We love because He first loved us" (1 John 4:19 ESV). We love Him as our very precious and exquisite pearl because He first loved us as His very precious and exquisite pearl.

If Jesus has loved and honored His bride like a pearl, how could we judge her? How could we judge ourselves? He climbed up a mountain and taught His followers to not be critics or judges of people. For the measure you use for others will be the same measure to you (Matthew 7:2). The measure you have within yourself will manifest in the way you measure others.

He went on to say, "Do not give dogs what is holy, and do not throw your pearls before pigs, lest they trample them underfoot and turn to attack you" (Matthew 7:6 ESV). Your voice, the sound of who and Whose you are, is the pearl. Do you throw your voice before dogs and pigs?

During the editing process of this book the Lord sat me before this passage. I was wrestling with the vulnerability of my message. Some of my most personal and intimate stories poured out on paper for people to receive as they will. I felt afraid that my best would be trampled underfoot. I was confused when He brought me to this passage because it looked to me like it validated the fear. I waited until I heard. *"I never threw my pearls before dogs or pigs. I threw Myself before My people - My pearl. My prize. My bride. I saw her as worth it. Do you think she is worth it?"*

I began to see flashes of heroes in our faith giving their absolute best, without reservation to the people of God. Stephen, in Acts 7 is one of my favorites. He threw pearls, the best of who he was, before religious leaders and they stoned him in response. Saul, who would become the apostle Paul, was in the crowd when Stephen spoke his last words with a loud voice. "Lord, do not hold this sin against them" (Acts 7:60 ESV). Stephen saw Saul as worth it when he was murdering believers.

On the brink of being stoned to death, Stephen gazed into heaven and saw Jesus standing at the right hand of God (Acts 7:55). The King of all kings was up and out of His eternal seat, ready to welcome a hero home. Success in the Kingdom is not measured by what people do in response to your pearls. Success is measured by what Jesus does. Critics looked at Stephen and shook their head, "He should've taken his pearls and went home." Jesus looked at Stephen and gave him a standing ovation.

If you see yourself like a dirty dog or unclean pig, you will see the world around you in the same way and will live with fearful restraint. If you see yourself as the pearl Jesus gave all to purchase, you will see a world that is worth the whole of your voice, without reservation.

> We look away from the natural realm and we fasten our gaze onto Jesus who birthed faith within us and who leads us forward into faith's perfection. His example is this: Because His heart was focused on the joy of knowing that you would be his, he endured the agony of the cross and conquered its humiliation, and now sits exalted at the right hand of the throne of God.
>
> Hebrews 12:2 TPT

Dirt Lid

The war on your voice is to keep you silent and reserved like a bride who measures herself as a dirty dog or unclean pig. Dirt becomes a lid in your life when it is defining you, instead of the Voice of the Bridegroom who found and wanted you to be His. When we treat the dirt like secrets that deserve to be hidden under lids, our voice becomes buried. He bought all the dirt in the field and the pearl. Your entire story has worth in the redemption of Jesus.

I first learned that secrets bury the purest sound of who and Whose we are in the same season where I saw myself as that dirty bride. I met Christel Wilson and a thousand hidden lids slowly began lifting just because she stepped into my life. Jesus often hides the sound of our breakthrough in the voice of those beside us. She had a depth of authentic, pure, and powerful love that to this day, has been one of the most profound influences in my story.

One night, when I was about nineteen, we set time aside to walk through an inner healing prayer session. She prayed at one point that what I needed to share would be brought to the front of my eyes. Everything had been blank until suddenly, memories popped up that felt impossible to turn into words. In one of them, I was nine or so and saw pornography for the first time.

I sat silent with that all too familiar feeling of being strangled inside, unable to speak. I unknowingly decided the places in my heart that felt dirty didn't deserve to be heard. They deserved to remain buried as secrets under a dirt lid.

Christel became the patience of Jesus for me. She waited for hours. She waited past the lie that says some things are so gross, they deserve to stay locked up inside. When all I could see was dirt, she saw a pearl that was worth her time.

I'll never forget the moment when I finally spoke out the memories I was seeing. I felt the weight of the dirt lid I had been living under lift off my life. Light came in. I was visible and still worthy of love. Secrets hide the truth of our value.

Years later, my entire world crashed into another dark, dirt lid. Christel was still there, sitting by my side. Confusion over intimacy and pain from unhealed wounds was closing in on my soul, until I was left feeling like

I could not breathe. Homosexual thoughts began tormenting my mind in a way I never knew was possible. No matter what I did or where I went, I couldn't escape all the chaos racing in my mind. I felt dirty, powerless, and stuck. My greatest fear was that the thoughts would overcome me and I would feel torment the rest of my life.

My whole world went dark under what felt like ten thousand dirt lids. In the lowest moment, I looked at pornography. I let a dead thing minister to the needs in my heart. When we expose our greatest vulnerability and needs to something that can't exchange life, we are left worse off than we began. It felt like years of breaking through lids was undone as I sat feeling stuck like that dirty, worn and unwanted bride.

Live in the Light

I knew this time, that the only thing to do was trust the deep work of real relationship lived in the Light. I sat beside Christel and my husband with dirt and shame piled so high, I could barely see anything true and right, but I knew under it all was a part of my heart that was worth living with nothing to hide. "But God proves His love for us in this: While we were yet sinners, Christ died for us" (Romans 5:8).

In our lowest moment, He treated us as a pearl who was worth it. It is the power of the gospel that makes room for us to sit beside the dirtiest places in our own soul and whisper, "You're not gross." When we can say it without a measure of judgment in our own soul, then we can sit beside a hurting, dirty world and whisper the hope of the Gospel that sees a pearl who is worth it.

Light doesn't always articulate answers and it rarely sounds profound. Light does this one thing extremely well; it sees the dirty places as much as the pretty and doesn't want any of it to hide. Light is that vulnerable place that requires great courage. That place where the cruelty of shame has a place to heal. Living in the light is living in real relationship, with nothing hiding under a secret lid. The truth of you is visible.

My husband could've picked up a stone. He could've grabbed a shovel and buried me deeper in the dark pit of despair. Instead, he became to me the Jesus I couldn't see. He drew close to the truth I was sharing. He knelt down until there was dirt on his knees.

Our Bridegroom Jesus came as the Light of the whole world and hid you inside Himself. You are hidden inside the brightest Light the world has ever seen. When you are hidden inside of Light, it's not so there is less to see. Your voice is not destined to be buried under lids, hiding in shadows or covered in fig leaves. You are safest and positioned to live free when exposed and undone inside the brightest Light of our redeeming Bridegroom King.

Light isn't in a hurry and doesn't have a need to cover up what's been done. When the Pharisees threw the adulteress woman at His feet, He didn't swoop her up and hide her away so she wouldn't feel embarrassed at what had been done. He took time to kneel down and write some unknown note with his finger, right beside her shame undone in the dirt.

One at a time, the people walked away and she waited at His feet. She met Mercy that saw her secrets. His nearness could absorb every unclean, gross thing. Jesus said, "Go and sin no more" (John 8:11). She was no longer a dirty person that would go and try to live clean. She was a pearl, redeemed by Light shining His grace on the darkest places of her soul. He was the end of her shame and the beginning of a new day in her story.

Real Identity

You are not your dirt. You are not your thoughts or cravings. You are not defined by the trauma in your past, your poor choices or tumultuous feelings. You are in a war to be the *real* you, your *real* voice. Your most authentic identity is not the first one that feels true.

The real you is absolutely called to thrive inside a life of holiness and purity, but truly living clean starts on the inside. When the inside of a cup is clean, then the outside will be clean as well. Jesus taught that it's no longer just about not committing adultery on the outside. It's about the hidden desires and thoughts on the inside (Matthew 5:28, 23:26). When we are stuck in sin patterns, we have to look inside the cup.

What makes us holy will be what keeps us holy. Our own performance, striving, and work to be squeaky clean will never be enough to live in true holiness. Jesus made us clean, white as snow. If you believe you are dirty, you will live dirty and make choices below your true identity. Clean people live a clean life because it's not something we do, but it's who we've become inside the spotless, perfect and holy Lamb of God.

Who are you without secrets, dirt and shame? The blood of Jesus has made sure you will find out. Believing the Gospel is believing the truest you is the one Jesus bought and made brand new. None of the scary stuff, none of the sin or lids are bigger than the resurrected nature of Christ inside of you.

Kris Vallotton of Bethel Church, taught messages on soul health and fear that were profoundly helpful in navigating the homosexual thoughts, perversion and pain that felt wildly bigger than me in that season.[1] He told a story of an intense time of torment where a demon showed up at the foot of his bed every night, leaving him sweating his bed wet with fear and anxiety. One night, still afraid, he looked at the demon and said, "Oh. It's only you," and rolled over. That was the night everything shifted in his season.

I had to make my way to becoming unimpressed with the magnitude of the thoughts and desires I was experiencing. The less impressed I was, the less influence they had over my mind. I began to see and believe I'm always free in Christ to choose how I'll respond to whatever is hurled my way. One moment and one thought at a time, I was learning to live in the Light of the Bridegroom.

In the same season, I had a vision of my heart – large, puffy and swollen. A needle came and pierced it, causing fluid to pour out. A thin, transparent, little heart was left naked and bare. Jesus gently put it in His hands. Staring intently with a cherishing look in His eye, He said, "This is my heart." I could see and feel that He loved it as His very own. I was His pearl.

As I shared the vision with my friend who was an EMT for years, she described how our physical hearts fill with liquid as a protective response to a traumatic experience. If the fluid isn't drained, it will actually crush the heart. What was meant to protect it can kill it.

Naked and unashamed in the hands of our Creator is our design. When we see the needle coming our way, it is Love coming to drain away everything we are not. The weight of protecting ourselves crushes the life out of us. He is the Protector that pierces through to defend what is true.

It's safe to be vulnerable, visible, and transparent, cradled there in His hands and covered by His smile. We no longer hide from our dirt, thoughts, pain or people. We hide inside of a *Person*. His affection protects us from the blows of rejection and arrows of fear. His kindness keeps us no matter what perversion swells up in the soul. We belong to Him. He defines us. We have no permission to believe anything else that tries to tell us it's not true.

An Exquisite Pearl

A woman named Mary who was a known prostitute heard that Jesus was reclining at a Pharisee's house named Simon (Luke 7:36-50). She had a story we don't know, but we do know little girls don't wake up one day with the dream of being a prostitute.

In my own personal story, I remember as a young girl, having fleeting desires to be in some sort of provocative career. It would never show up on the "what do you want to be when you grow up" dream list, but scenarios where my body was wanted would randomly flash through my mind. The sexual abuse in my story was confusing my value.

The first, most obvious boundary that defines and sets you apart as unique is your body. It's easy to see where you end and someone else begins when you look at the way we've all been given an individual body. When that first and most natural physical boundary is violated, it sends a message that your value begins and ends with what your body can offer. What you can offer with your physical body cannot fulfill and sustain the eternal need in your heart to be seen, loved and cherished as individual you. My healthy needs to feel seen, wanted, and known were confused. Sexual confusion was value and intimacy confusion.

The height of true, real worth and intimacy is not sexual. Our most intimate connection and place of absolute value are with our God and that connection will never be sexual. Somewhere in Mary's unknown story, she discovered her real worth. She heard the Voice of her Bridegroom. She discovered He didn't see a dirty dog, unclean pig, or unwanted bride when He saw her. He saw a pearl worth buying the whole field for and He, in turn, became her pearl.

She wasn't thinking like a dirty prostitute when she decided to show up to Simon's house uninvited to bring something of worth to Jesus. She walked straight through the door and knelt behind the feet of Jesus. She broke an alabaster flask of ointment and began weeping. Her tears and the ointment poured over the dirty feet of Jesus. She wiped His feet clean and kissed them over and over.

Simon couldn't believe Jesus was letting a prostitute touch Him. He believed her sexual dirt should keep her away. He was confused about worth and intimacy. Jesus had some feedback for Simon in story form. Jesus said one debtor owed 500 denarii and one owed fifty. They were both forgiven, but who would love more? The one with the larger debt will love that master more.

Jesus turned towards the woman and said to Simon,

> Do you see this woman? I entered your house; you gave me no water
> for my feet, but she has wet my feet with her tears and wiped them
> with her hair. You gave me no kiss, but from the time I came in she
> has not ceased to kiss my feet. You did not anoint my head with oil,
> but she has anointed my feet with ointment. Therefore I tell you, her
> sins, which are many, are forgiven-for she loved much. But he who is
> forgiven little, loves little.

Luke 7:44-47 ESV

Our passion for Jesus is directly connected to our awareness of our need
for the forgiveness of Jesus. The one who has been forgiven of much, loves
much. We don't stir up love for Him. We are propelled toward extravagant
love as we see and receive His extravagant love and forgiveness for us.

Mary threw all her worship before Jesus and didn't allow the opinions of others
to bury the sound of her love for Him. We won't always have a place at Simon's
table, but we will always have a place at the feet of Jesus. Simon didn't think she
was worthy to be in the room, let alone touching Jesus. He was full of pride and
judgement yet Mary didn't wait until Simon wasn't in the room to pour out her
most intimate worship to Jesus. She apparently saw Simon as worthy of being
in the room as she gave her best to Jesus. When you know the debt you were
forgiven, you know He is rich enough in grace for anyone to be forgiven.

She wasn't a dirty, unwanted dog walking into a room uninvited. She was a
very precious and exquisite pearl Jesus gave up all to buy for an extraordinary
price. She was the sound of His redeemed bride walking into the room.

True freedom from the fear of man is living "glorious and radiant, beautiful and holy, without fault or flaw" in unreserved passion for Jesus

because He forgave us. We are no longer funneling our thoughts through an internal measure of critics and judgments. Mary didn't wait until her reputation had changed to live the uninhibited sound of who and Whose she was. Her reputation changed because she no longer gave herself to her reputation. The whole of her voice was given and poured out before her Bridegroom.

Oil of Intimacy

Intimacy with our Bridegroom will always be the motive that moves our life forward, the oil that causes our fire to burn bright. In Matthew 25, Jesus said the Kingdom of Heaven was like ten virgins who took their lamps and went to meet the bridegroom. Five were wise and brought oil and five were foolish and did not. The oil that causes our fire to burn is as important as the fire itself. The motive that moves us forward is as important as the direction we are going.

The bridegroom was delayed and all ten became drowsy and slept. They woke up to the cry, "He is here!" The oil wasn't an issue until they woke from rest and realized their fire needed attention through the delay.

The fire is for the Bridegroom's presence and the oil of intimacy is the only thing that endures through the twists, turns, discouragements and challenges of delay. The lamps of the wise burned brighter after rest. Without oil, the others burnt out. What happens in rest points to the oil fueling our fire. Intimacy burns bright in rest. Judgment, religion, fear of man – none of those oils can make it through the night.

They trimmed their lamps and the foolish virgins asked for more oil. The wise virgins said, "No." Of all the things we can share and generously give away, the oil of intimacy is not one of them. Relationship is personal. No one can know someone for you. A lamp can light the way for many, but it can only light up the whole face for one. Intimacy is face to face.

The only way to know if we're staying warm by someone else's fire, hiding in the shadow of someone else's relationship, is to rest in the mundane of our life. When the exciting meetings end, the busyness is pulled back to rest and we are being faithful in the invisible, little things, who do we become? If our oil runs out, we know it's time to cultivate and tend to the fire in the most significant place of our life – our own soul.

The most significant eyes on our life are not the ones from big crowds or even the tiny eyes of our little kids in tow. It's our invisible God who sees the deep of our life and whose relationship alone is to be our most intimate home. Of all the places we live loud in the uninhibited sound of our voice, home with Him is the loudest.

His

On June 8th, 2002, I wore a pure white wedding dress and walked down the rose-petaled isle looking 100 percent opposite of the vision I'd had at fifteen. Of all the thousands of things I loved about that day, one overwhelming memory swallows up all the others – the look on my bridegroom's face. He had a ridiculous happiness coming through his bright blue eyes. They were a little bit glazed over, completely undone in love. I was his and he was happy. The perfect dress, first dance and gorgeous cake all pale next to the memory of his happiness. My bridegroom was and is the best part of being a bride.

To this day, he still gets that look on his face. Of all the things I get to do and be while on the earth, being his is my favorite part of life. The excellent wife in Proverbs 31, "smiled at her future" (31:25 NASB). I think she was smiling because she was trusting her husband would be there.

How much eternally more reason in Jesus do we have to smile at our future? He will be there. Just the sound of His voice by His bride was enough to complete John's joy. Whatever is left wanting in your joy is filled by hearing the Voice of the Bridegroom. There is not a happier place to be than on His arm, living by His side as His bride. The best part of being the voice of a bride that's "glorious and radiant, beautiful and holy, without fault or flaw" is being His.

When we live as the pearl in the Light of our Bridegroom, we can't help but discover that dreams do come true.

Chapter 8
Dreams Do Come True

THE MAJORITY OF my childhood was dedicated to a bald-headed, flimsy, plastic baby that was ever on my hip. I spent endless hours whisked away in the dream of love. My fake husband was practically perfect in every way. He would go away for the day and I would be busy building a fire out of wild calla-lilies and setting a table of leaves and things until everything was just right. I created home. I played family again and again. It never grew old. I was happiest when all my little life was poured out playing the dream of my someday.

Cinderella was my favorite. The way she flung wide the curtains in her tiny room and gazed at the distant castle with twinkling eyes. She sang to the birds and dreamed of love. She was so kind. The prince, lifting his eyes at the ball and being caught by her beauty got me every time. The rest of the room went dim and all his attention was fixed on her like she was the only one in the crowd. When the movie came to an end, I always wondered about happily ever after. I always wished the story was longer.

No one teaches a child to dream or pretend. It's wired within us. Jesus redeemed the process of childhood. He could have stepped out of heaven at thirty-three. Like Adam and Eve, He could've skipped the toddler and teen years, but He didn't. He started in a womb and grew like every other little boy and girl. I often wonder what He did with sticks and the dreams that fueled pretend play in His childhood.

Culturally, thirty was quite old. He was way behind the times for marriage and kids. His mom initiated his first public miracle at the wedding when He was at rest and present in His season. We never see Him in a hurry or motivated by an urgency of feeling behind. He took time to grow slow from infancy into the One who could deliver and sustain the dream that was to come.

Winning the war on your voice requires that you dream dreams and take time to become the person who can live within them. The people beside you now and the ones you will never meet are impacted by what you choose to do with the dream of your voice. The uninhibited sound of who and Whose you are isn't just for now, the next season or your lifetime. Your voice is for eternity.

Delight in the Land

Our dreams are to propel us into paying a price in the war to become the person who can live in the dream. The people of God stepped inside the borders of their Promised Land – the grapes, the honey, the milk, the land of their dreams – and they missed the joy of it. Psalm 106:24b-25 describes it like this, "They despised the land of delight you gave to them. They grumbled and found fault with everything and closed their hearts to your voice" (TPT).

The reality inside them couldn't sustain delight in the land the Lord gave them. It is possible for your voice to despise, grumble and find only fault with a land that was once the sweetest dream. The land is a gift from the Lord, but to be the person that can live inside the land takes growth.

Caring for a plastic baby with delight is an entirely different experience than caring for a real one with delight. Being a happy wife was easy when it was just a dream. When we look around our lives, we can always find something we are currently living in that used to be a dream we looked forward to with happy expectation.

If you can't find one, start with driving. When you were twelve it was probably the overwhelming dream on your mind; being in control of where you go, using the blinker and pedals. It was wildly exciting until it became super familiar. How easy it becomes to grumble and find fault with every crazy driver out there in rush hour traffic. We owe it to our twelve year-old selves to be grateful drivers!

One day the Lord interrupted the grumbling and complaining in my mind. *"I brought you here to bless you. Lift up your head."*

His intention is always good. He brought you to your relationships, your job and the season you're in to bless you and fulfill dreams or prepare you to live the dreams in your heart. Our internal reality determines what we see and our capacity to either despise the land with our voice or delight in it.

In Numbers 13:2, God clearly said, "Send men to spy out the land of Canaan, which I am giving to the people of Israel" (ESV).

The greatest wrestle wasn't over the land being theirs, but the capacity within them to receive and walk in the reality of what God had given them. They seemed to themselves like grasshoppers next to the giants (Numbers 13:33). Don't exhaust yourself questioning if what God has promised will be true in your life. Instead, focus on your voice becoming bigger than a grasshopper's on the inside so you can carry the reality of the promise and delight in it.

It's impossible to live within the boundary of your promised land without boundaries. I have a huge value for boundaries because I have a huge value and giant responsibility to protect delight in my land. Boundaries aren't first about what I'm keeping out, but what I want to keep in – in my gaze, heart and life. Delight is an inside job and boundaries help us to keep delight in the reality of our dreams.

All of the spies saw the same giants and grapes within the boundary of the land, but only Joshua and Caleb were able to keep the goodness and the promise of their God as the overwhelming reality. They had boundaries within them that chose what they would focus on in the pursuit of the dream. Understanding that we choose what we magnify in our life is a huge part of growing bigger than a grasshopper inside.

If you find yourself despising your life, grumbling about things that used to be a dream, finding unending fault in the people and places God has given you, we've all been there but never have to stay there. Look to the magnifying glass that is ever in your hand. Grow into the person who can sustain a blown-up gaze on "whatever is true, whatever is honorable, whatever is just, whatever is pure, whatever is lovely, whatever is commendable, excellent and worthy of praise" (Philippians 4:8). Be the one who sees the giants, yet chooses to use your voice to magnify the grapes and His faithful goodness.

The Real Thing

There is not a greater dream to magnify than the dream of our God. Jesus is the desire of all nations (Haggai 2.7 KJV). Ten thousand dreams fulfilled will never be enough to fill us up if the desire for Jesus is not satisfied. I have found that the fulfillment of even the sweetest dream cannot satisfy the deepest ache and desire in my heart for the Presence of God. My heart sinks when I hear of people in my nation at the height of their dream job, in their dream house with their dream family ending their life with suicide. The earth is groaning for hope. Nations are dreaming of a fulfillment found only in Jesus. The voice of sons and daughters living inside the presence of Jesus with satisfied desire releases the hope that dreams do come true.

I saw the significance of real fulfillment one afternoon at the mall while we were taking a play break at the slides. The pretzel shop was strategically positioned in plain sight at every angle of the happy, play place. The smell of the freshly baking pretzels was definitely overpowering all the kid smells flying down slides.

I watched at a distance as my toddler lifted her head from her focused waddling. She was awestruck by a blinking cardboard pretzel that was bigger than her body. Without hesitating, she darted for the pretzel. She stood in front of it in awe. I was watching at a distance, curious. She leaned over and licked the cardboard pretzel! Confused, she did it again. The third time, I started walking over to swoop up my disappointed girl.

It looked and smelled like a pretzel, but it was definitely not a pretzel. She could've walked away believing pretzels taste like terrible cardboard for the rest of her toddler life and cynically said, "Been there, done that," whenever someone started talking about how incredibly wonderful a pretzel is.

You actually have to step up to the counter and pay a real price for a real pretzel. A real pretzel with a toddler is a real mess. The cinnamon and sugar get all over. The sticky little fingers and crumb-stained face are proof she's had the real thing. She's smiling wide and asking for more before she's even finished. Squeaky clean, disappointing cardboard pretzels can't bring an authentic, satisfied smile to her face.

Real relationship with a real God feels messy and deeply satisfying at the exact same time. What a tragedy when we settle for a cardboard Jesus, believing He's disappointing and unfulfilling because of what we *tried* several times. Not all roads lead to relationship with the real, authentic Jesus. It's a narrow road. It costs our entire life. You can't *try* giving Him your everything.

It's not a sad thing to step up to the counter when you know what you're getting in exchange. You don't grumble and complain when you know what is coming is worth eternally more than what you just paid. The apostle Paul called everything He gave up garbage compared to knowing Christ (Philippians 3:8). If He feels disappointing and we've become cynical, squeaky clean and unchanged, we need to step up to the counter and pay a price to live in real fulfillment.

A life of faith is not waiting for Jesus to show up for us, like licking that cardboard pretzel and believing someday it will turn into a real one. A life of faith bows before Him and gives our entire life because we believe He already did show up for us. Of all the things we wait for in our faith, Immanuel, God with us, is not one of them. He came. Real relationship costs our control, pride, and tendency to hide. We lay down our dependence on rules and any walls we've built isolating us from the need to trust Him. Trusting Him without control often feels messy.

The cry for more doesn't spill out from our heart because we are starving, unfulfilled or disappointed. We cry for more with sticky fingers and a messy face because we have tasted and seen and are now ruined for anything but real, beautiful and satisfying Jesus.

Live the Real Story

Living in real, fulfilling relationship with Jesus requires that we live inside our real story. I saw a real story when we took our girls to Disney World for the first time. We were excited to whisk them away to the happiest place on earth. It's so magical seeing it through their eyes. We met princess after princess and my four little girls lit up.

We came to Cinderella and I watched with joy. She was still my favorite. This time I was old enough to look in her eyes. Behind the fancy dress, sparkling shoes, crown and smile, I saw a person with pain inside. She gets paid to pretend. She works to make a fairy tale come to life.

Living every day in the happiest place on earth can't put happiness deep inside if every night you take off your mask and put your gown aside. None of the smiles, adoration and cheers can be personally fulfilling if we're pretending. Religion pushes us to pretend to be worth loving. The real Gospel bends down to the most worthless places in our story and whispers, "You're Mine."

Your entire story is destined to be the sound of hope that dreams do, indeed, come true. I felt the truth of that sound one night in worship preparing to give a last charge to graduating BASSM students. I was telling the Lord I wanted to give them the best of me as they finished their year. I was waiting to hear what I might share. I saw Him smile and point to one of the worst moments of my life. My heart started to race. I wanted to share a powerful revelation or impart some gift He'd placed on my life. He wanted to open up the well of mercy that ran deepest and most real in my life.

We give the best of who we are by giving from the truth of who we are. In the lowest places of our lives, we are just as qualified because the same grace is sustaining our weaknesses *and* our strengths. Our crown isn't something we take off and on; it's who we have become. While we were yet sinners, the King gave us His life and adopted us as His own (Romans 5:8). You wear the same crown in your failure as you do in your success, because you will never be more or less of a child of the King.

I shared a story of complete failure in the charge to the students that night with a shaky voice and sweaty palms. I felt another layer of shame in my own life fall to the ground and I watched chains of shame all across the room break loose over the people Jesus so loved. When we live *naked and unashamed* in the truth of our story, the beauty of Jesus can't help but be savored and seen. If my voice only reveals the highlight reel, the most people will ever see is me. If my voice reveals my need for a Savior in every season of the story, people will see a Jesus that is infinitely bigger than me.

Zephaniah 3:19 says, "I will change their shame into praise and renown in all the earth." Shame turns into praise when we think like He thinks about every area of our life. Happily ever after isn't a shattered dream. Happily ever after is a Bridegroom King spreading wide His arms on a tree, paying the price for a crown of joy to forever rest on our victorious heads.

Hope is not a fantasy. Fantasy is a dream that never paid a price. Fantasy longs for fulfillment without laying down one's life. There is no cost to fantasy because it's tucked away within the protection of our imagination. It's a relationship that's not real. Fantasy can relieve the pain of a deficit in the moment, but it's cardboard to the soul. There are no nutrients. There's no real, alive, intimate love moving us towards our dreams.

Fantasy wishes for a life that is not our own and becomes an escape from the real world around us. It writes a story that's fiction. True hope is attached to our present reality and future dreams at the exact same time. Hope creates space to feel and see the deficits in our lives. The pain, disappointments, lack and reality of our history are all included when Hope writes our future story. Hope is an intimate exchange because it depends on the God of all hope as our source. Hope requires trust, vulnerability and faith. Hope is deeply relational. It is the joyful and eager expectation of good coming around the corner because we vulnerably trust in the nature of our good God.

Promised Land without Measure

Whatever page your real story is on, Jesus wrote in a promise for you before He went to the cross. He gave us the promise of the Holy Spirit without measure (John 3:34, 14:16). His goodness will be searched out for all eternity and still be found without measure. In Canaan, the land had huge grapes, flowing milk, and honey. In the Holy Spirit, we have the entire Kingdom of Heaven.

"For the kingdom of God is not a matter of eating and drinking but of righteousness and peace and joy **in the Holy Spirit**" (Romans 14:7 ESV emphasis added).

No matter how much we've tasted and seen, there will always be more unexplored, fulfilling promised land inside of Him. I was reminded of this truth when I stumbled downstairs early the other morning. It was still dark and I was making coffee with one sleepy eye open. We have a new beautiful, water filter in the laundry room. I headed that way, true to my morning routine of filling up a glass of water.

I turned the water on and as it poured into the bottom of the glass, the bottom fell off. It was so odd. The bottom just fell out. Water was rushing through the bottomless cup and I heard the Holy Spirit say, *"There is no bottom to Me and there will be no bottom to you."*

When we use this phrase, *the bottom fell out,* in our culture, it denotes a loss of value. It speaks of a structure of measure falling apart. In the Kingdom, when the bottom falls out, it's our invitation to live without containment. God has no measure, no beginning and no end. His value is unending and in Him, ours is too.

"Believe in me so that rivers of living water will burst out from within you, flowing from your innermost being, just like the Scripture says!" Jesus was prophesying about the Holy Spirit that believers were being prepared to receive" (John 7:38-39b TPT).

We are not vessels that contain His Presence. We are the bottomless cup bursting forth Living Water that will never run dry. In 2 Kings 4, there's a story of vessels of oil that helps us see our invitation into the endless supply in the Holy Spirit. Elisha was helping a poor widow save her sons from being taken away as slaves. He first asked her, "What do you have in the house?" She answered, "Your servant has nothing in the house except a jar of oil."

The conversation in the Kingdom always begins with what we do have. When it feels like we're not living in the abundant and supernatural supply promised, all the things we don't have want to shout for our attention. Heaven is asking us to look for what we *do* have. The widow had a jar of oil.

Elisha told her to go to all her neighbors and borrow as many vessels as she could and pour her oil into the vessels. When the vessels were full, she said to her son, "Bring me another vessel." And he said to her, "There is not another." Then the oil stopped flowing.

In that moment when the oil dried up, she didn't regret gathering as many as she could. I've never heard anyone say, "I'm so glad I doubted the Lord." I'm sure she wished she had more vessels! She valued what she had in the natural and then prepared in faith for increase through a miracle.

She stepped into supernatural supply, but the oil stopped flowing when the vessels ran out. We are the vessels with no bottom and no lid, whose capacity never runs out. In us, the oil of the Holy Spirit flows without end and without measure like a rushing river. When "the bottom falls out," our voice as living vessels of His Presence, comes alive. The widow's dream in this story was the freedom of her sons. We, too, are taking risks, believing God and extending the borders of our land in Him so that our sons and daughters will benefit. Living with eternity in mind means living with dreams that will benefit sons and daughters we will never see.

100-Year Vision

Hezekiah was a wildly successful king who in the end, missed living with his sons and daughters in mind. In 2 Kings 20, he was miraculously healed on his deathbed and granted fifteen more years of life. The king of Babylon came and brought gifts to honor Hezekiah.

Hezekiah welcomed them and he showed them all his treasure house, the silver, the gold, the spices, the precious oil, his armory, all that was found in his storehouses. There was nothing in his house or in all his realm that Hezekiah did not show them (2 Kings 20:13 ESV).

Isaiah then came and gave Hezekiah a heart-wrenching word that Babylon would carry away all the wealth that had been stored up and even his own sons would be taken away to the palace of the king of Babylon. Hezekiah, sadly, rested in the word. "For he thought, 'Why not, if there will be peace and security in my days?' " (2 Kings 20:19b ESV).

Hezekiah experienced an overwhelming amount of dreams that came true and made a stunning mark in his hour of history, but missed who the dreams were to benefit. He showed off his wealth as his own instead of living like it belonged to sons and daughters he would never see. About one hundred years after Isaiah prophesied those words, King Nebuchadnezzar from Babylon came to Jerusalem and besieged it (Daniel 1:1). Daniel was one of Hezekiah's extraordinary sons who was taken into the king of Babylon's palace. Hezekiah's dreams of peace and security didn't reach a hundred years down the road into Daniel's day.[1]

Matthew 6:19 tells us to lay up treasure in heaven for where our treasure is, our heart will be also. The greatest, most fulfilling dreams can't be measured in storehouses, silver or gold, but in eternal reward. When our heart is in heaven, earthly measure is not impressive. The greatest reward in winning the war on your voice can't be seen in your lifetime. Dream dreams for your voice that impact the Daniel's you will never meet, but are impacted by the choices you make. In one hundred years, I pray your freedom, your dreams, and the sound of your laughter finds your sons and daughters.

> When the Lord restored the fortunes of Zion, we were like those who dream. Then our mouth was filled with laughter, and our tongue with shouts of joy; then they said among the nations, "The Lord has done great things for us; we are glad.
>
> Psalm 126:1-3 ESV

Real Reward

I love to look back at that wide-eyed little girl in my childhood, giving all her days to a pretend husband, and smile. I love to remember what moved her heart. I love to show her dreams do come true; promises are fulfilled and hope is not a fantasy. I love to show up in the dream and pay the price to be who she always dreamed of being.

When so much of society and circumstance, pain and disappointment are grumbling that the dream is not real or worth it and the fairy tale is fake, I love to step back in time and watch her dream without limits. I love to bend down to her bright-eyed imagination and remember her playing her deepest wish.

I pull back her stringy, long hair and whisper in her little ear: *You are worth it. You are enough. Your dream is enough. You will smile. You will laugh. You will cry. You will be loyal, faithful and pure. You will never stop starting. You will get back up again, again. You will stay soft. You will be relentlessly kind. You will be full of grace and truth. Your dreams will come overwhelmingly true. You will be a happy wife. Living your real story is better than your best day of play. You are innocent and full of faith. You will stay that way. You will live without measure and without a lid. You will live aware of who and Whose you are. You will have a powerful voice.*

After I go back to the beginning, I love to close my eyes and go all the way to the end of my lifetime. I get up close to see the wrinkles on my wrinkles. I lived entirely spent. There's nothing left in me. I gave it all in love. Jesus received His full reward in me.

I picture myself squeezing my daughter's tiny granddaughter and look beyond what I will ever live to see. Up and down, through life's every twist and turn, the goodness of God will have no end. She will see, we don't live from the ever changing circumstances in our story looking for His goodness. We live inside His unchanging goodness and from there, move towards the reality of our story. There's no pain too deep for the love of God to reach. Nothing is impossible for one life laid at the feet of such a wild, Bridegroom King. She will find He's so much better than she could ever dream. He is her desire, satisfied.

I breathe in who she is and smile, knowing I fought battles in this war that she will never have to fight. I have blood stains ever on my sword and handing victory to her is my reward. I lived with her in mind. Her children's children may never know my laugh or call out my name, but they will benefit from the way I lived.

I pull back that stringy, long hair and whisper in her little ear: *You are worth it. You are enough. Your dream is enough. You will smile. You will laugh. You will cry. You will be loyal, faithful and pure. You will never stop starting. You will get back up again, again. You will stay soft. You will be relentlessly kind. You will be full of grace and truth. Your dreams will come overwhelmingly true. You will be a happy wife. Living your real story is better than your best day of play. You are innocent and full of faith. You will stay that way. You will live without measure and without a lid. You will live aware of who and Whose you are. You will have a powerful voice.*

End Notes

Introduction

1. @OnWritingDaily (Allen Ginsberg) "To gain your own voice, you have to forget about having it heard." *Twitter, 13 Jul. 2017, 2:04 p.m.* https://twitter.com/OnWritingDaily/status/885605954594754564

Chapter 1

1. See lovingonpurpose.com for Danny Silk resources.

Chapter 2

1. See brilliantbookhouse.com, "The Process Series," for Graham Cooke's teaching on this.

Chapter 3

1. C. Austin Miles. Lyrics to "In the Garden." Wikipedia, 2018. https://en.wikipedia.org/wiki/In_the_Garden_(1912_song)
2. Guzik, David. "Study Guide for Daniel 1." Blue Letter Bible, 2013.
3. Guzik, David. "Study Guide for Daniel 3." Blue Letter Bible, 2013.
4. Leaf, Caroline. *Eat and Think Yourself Smart.* Baker Books, 2016. 123.

Chapter 4

1. Guzik, David. "Study Guide for Judges 6." Blue Letter Bible, 2017.

Chapter 6

1. See drleaf.com for resources by Caroline Leaf.

2. Guzik, David. "Study Guide for John 13." Blue Letter Bible, 2017.

3. Guzik, David. "Study Guide for Exodus 21." Blue Letter Bible, 2017.

Chapter 7

1. See shop.bethel.com for resources by Kris Vallotton on fear and soul health.

Chapter 8

1. Guzik, David. "Study Guide for 2 Kings 20." Blue Letter Bible, 2017

Recommended Reading

- *Healing the Orphan Spirit* by **Leif Hetland**
- *Angel's Song* by **Jennifer Hetland**
- *Keep Your Love On* by **Danny Silk**
- *Cracks in the Foundation* by **Steve Backlund**
- *Victorious Emotions* by **Wendy Backlund**
- *God is Good* by **Bill Johnson**
- *The Veil* by **Blake Healy**
- *The Supernatural Ways of Royalty* by **Kris Vallotton**
- *Words of Knowledge Made Easy* by **Scott Thompson**
- *Coming Into Alignment* by **Graham Cooke**
- *The Conversation in Heaven* by **Abigail Holt-Jennings**
- *Kisses from a Good God* by **Paul Manwaring**
- *Rooted* by **Banning Liebscher**
- *The God Zone* by **Sherri Lewis**
- *Switch on Your Brain* by **Caroline Leaf**
- *Birthing the Miraculous* by **Heidi Baker**
- *The Happy Intercessor* by **Beni Johnson**